THE BASIS OF CHRISTIAN PRAYER

THE BASIS OF CHRISTIAN PRAYER

H. P. OWEN

Late Emeritus Professor of Christian Doctrine
King's College, University of London

REGENT COLLEGE PUBLISHING
Vancouver, British Columbia

Published 2006 by Regent College Publishing
5800 University Boulevard, Vancouver, BC V6T 2E4 Canada
Web: www.regentpublishing.com
E-mail: info@regentpublishing.com

Regent College Publishing is an imprint of the Regent Bookstore
<www.regentbookstore.com>. Views expressed in works published
by Regent College Publishing are those of the author and do not
necessarily represent the official position of
Regent College <www.regent-college.edu>.

Library and Archives Canada Cataloguing in Publication Data

Owen, Huw Parri
The basis of Christian prayer / by H.P. Owen; foreword by
Stephen N. Williams.

Includes bibliographical references.
ISBN 1-57383-171-9

1. Prayer–Christianity. I. Title.

BV210.3.O93 2005   248.3'2   C2005-905637-1

CONTENTS

FOREWORD

Stephen N. Williams

In October, 1996, Huw Parri Owen, Emeritus Professor of Christian Doctrine at King's College, London, died just a few weeks short of his seventieth birthday. He was no ordinary man and no ordinary theologian. Raised in Cardiff, South Wales, he obtained a Scholarship to study at Jesus College, Oxford, at the end of the Second World War and proceeded to read Classics and Theology. His first teaching appointments were in Aberystwyth and Bangor, in Wales, where he concentrated on the New Testament, but when he moved to King's in 1961, it was to lecture in the history and philosophy of religion. When the Chair came along in 1970, it was in Christian Doctrine. It is tempting to suppose that the range of competence exhibited in these appointments was easier to attain then than it is now, given increased specialization. But, even at the time, it was a wider range than usual, and Huw Owen himself believed that from the students' point of view, his teaching in Christian Ethics was appreciated most of all. In 1981, he took early retirement in order to devote the remaining years of his life to reading, thinking and writing in theology, a life that was cut short by illness before there was any sign of diminution of his mental powers.

From a writing and publishing point of view, events took a rather unusual turn over the fifteen years of retirement. *Christian Theism* appeared in 1984, but that was the last full-length publication to emerge.[1] However, he wrote three books after that. The first was a study of Christianity and Platonism; typically bucking a widespread contemporary trend, Huw Owen thought that there were interesting and positive affinities here that deserved an unfashionable re-statement or fresh statement. The second was a broad-based treatment of the basis and nature of Christian belief. Although these were sent to publishers, they were not actually published and no copies were found amongst his literary remains. Almost certainly, he destroyed them.[2] But a third book was also completed and this alone was preserved in its author's characteristically meticulous handwriting. I shall not recount its odyssey from the day of his death to its publication here and now but this is the one that we publish—a gift, James Houston has said, to the Church of Jesus Christ.

Huw Parri Owen is less known now than he was two decades ago, when *Christian Theism* was published.[3] While he may have had his equals in clarity of thought and writing, he scarcely had his betters. Anyone who reads his published corpus will surely acknowledge it. *Revelation and Existence* remains a convincing critique of Bultmann's thought; *The Moral Argument for Christian Theism* was, in its day, as elegant a statement of its case as could be conceived; *Concepts of Deity* and *The Christian Knowledge of God*, the latter being his longest work, remain models of philosophical and theological precision.[4] With *Christian Theism*, he produced what he would himself call his 'mini-Summa', garnering and presenting the fruits of years of thought and teaching, and referring, in this phrase, to Aquinas' *Summa Theologiae*. (I am not sure whether Huw was conscious of the fact that Aquinas died at somewhere around the same age at which he published *Christian Theism!*) It is 'mini' indeed: the volume is economical to a fault. In so referring, however, Huw was not indulging in self-inflating boasting. On the contrary, he was the most self-deprecating and self-effacing of people. He found personal fulfilment not in travelling around and lecturing, but in the tranquillity of patient reflection. He was somewhat reclusive, particularly after retirement, when professional commitments ended. That he was a most gifted pianist was little known. It was not much better known, I suspect, that his older, musically-distinguished, half-sister married Freud's biographer, Ernest Jones.[5] In addition to the volumes that I have mentioned, Huw Parri Owen wrote a relatively little-known short book on W. R. Matthews entitled *W. R. Matthews: Philosopher and Theologian.*[6] The late Queen Mother was most interested in Matthews' work, but it was typical of Huw that he resisted attempts to persuade him to send her a copy, something which she would undoubtedly have appreciated and which would have elicited grateful correspondence from her.

I must stop here, sensing Huw's shadow squirming with embarrassment and acute irritation at all these personal references. So we turn to the present volume. Its title adequately conveys its substance and its text substantially reproduces his (literal) manuscript. Some of the punctuation has been amended, bibliographical detail has been filled out and the language made inclusive. Biblical quotations from the RSV have been retained even when the forms 'Thee' and 'Thou' appear because, in the course of this volume, the author briefly comments on that issue. Very occasionally indeed, I have made a minor phraseological alteration of the qualifying kind if something has seemed to me a trifle ambiguous. Huw himself might well have intended to carry out such minor revisions, had he lived. But, unsurprisingly, the work makes singularly few editorial demands on someone who has ended up as a species of unappointed literary executor.

In terms of its content, what is written presupposes theological convictions for which the author argues elsewhere, but not here. Two should be singled out because they dominate the exposition from the beginning. Firstly, the author was an uncompromising advocate of what is widely known as 'classical theism'. Readers who are uncertain of the ins and outs of the axioms of classical theism will find no better explanation of them than in Huw Parri Owen's own work, particularly *Concepts of Deity* and the first chapter of *Christian Theism*. Huw's tenacity on this point was unusual in one respect, I suspect. In *Christian Knowledge of God*, he had conceded that the chief point on which classical theism was vulnerable was in its ascription of impassibility to God—the belief, roughly stated, that God cannot suffer. He was then willing to defend the view that God feels pain.[7] But—and this is what I take to be unusual—at a time when denial of divine impassibility was to all appearances gaining ground, he moved in the opposite direction, back towards the more 'classical' position, although he did not arrive at any dogmatic conclusion on the question. It was Friedrich von Hugel's work that influenced him here.[8]

Readers who are not classical theists will therefore find themselves at odds with the author from near the beginning of this book. In this connection, it is probably appropriate to refer to 'open theism', which has been a live and emotive subject for many years now in North American evangelical circles. Gerald Bray has opined that the question of prayer lies right at the heart of open theists' concerns.[9] Whether or not we attach quite that weight to the question, it is indubitably important to them, and any contemporary treatment of prayer that aspires to include North American evangelicals amongst its constituent readership, but proceeds simply to assume classical theism, begs big questions. That is true, of course, for other readerships. Here, we must bear two things in mind. Firstly, the author had already defended classical theism (whether or not persuasively) elsewhere.[10] Secondly, he simply was not writing with open theism in mind and was doubtless unaware of its existence.[11]

The second set of assumptions are soteriological and can be picked up in his references to such things as the co-operation of the human with the divine will, sanctifying grace, virtue and perseverance. At points, he may be judged 'semi-Pelagian', using the phrase either neutrally or with pejorative intent, although perhaps that is inevitably to evaluate from a dogmatic traditional-Protestant standpoint and the description in any case may be judged inapplicable. However that may be, it is a position which the author expounded and defended elsewhere with his customary brevity.[12] If open theism has entered the lists in opposition to classical theism, it has more particularly opposed Calvinism too, and in that context we note that Huw Parri Owen was himself no fan of Calvinism. He worked right through Calvin's *Institutes* relatively late in his teaching career and, indeed, found himself in agreement with more in it than he supposed that he would.[13] However, he firmly rejected its soteriology. Augustinian predestination is flatly rejected in this present volume on prayer, as it is in his earlier work. Libertarian freedom—very roughly, our capacity to choose and to do freely otherwise than we actually do—was something of which he was firmly convinced, although his statement of that conviction is careful.[14] Personal agency and morality made absolutely no sense to him unless we maintained the reality of such a freedom. And his discussion of prayer is steered fully as much by this conviction as by classical theism, with equally decisive results for the theology of prayer.

It is not appropriate for me to foist on the reader personal judgements about issues such as these, involving assumptions that are defended in other volumes. But, as one who enjoyed friendship and several personal conversations with the author in what turned out to be the closing years of his life, I believe that Huw would not object if, at this point, I risk being inappropriately intrusive and 'conscientiously' register my demurral from some things in this volume, lest the reader assume that my introduction constitutes a straightforward commendation. 'Conscience' was a hallowed and sacred area on his view of it. So I shall mention three things.

Firstly, questions should be asked about the author's use of Scripture. I pass over here critical assumptions which come to light in the treatment of the differences between Matthew and Luke in their reports of the Lord's Prayer (chapter 4). Before we come to that discussion, Huw Owen discusses petition and intercession as forms of vocal prayer, in chapter 3. I shall let the reader find out for him or herself what his argument is here, but it will be noted that the author limits the scope of our petitions and questions the causal efficacy of intercessions in a way that many will find drastic and disturbing. It is important that we consider his arguments carefully for two connected reasons. Firstly, our prayers are often thoughtless. Secondly, they are based on unexamined assumptions about the nature of God, ourselves, and divine and human agency. On the first point, reflection on the actual argument and not just the conclusion presented in this volume will help banish our thoughtlessness. On the second, Huw Owen's arguments on petition and intercession are, as we have indicated, explicitly based on his own wider commitments on the nature of God and humanity, including on the significance of human free will. Yet it is important that we think critically not just about the author's conclusions, but about his approach.

The whole discussion actually well exemplifies the author's general theological method. He took the Bible seriously and reflected carefully on it. However, what we have in his discussion is not focussed on the records of the specific petitions and intercessions that crowd its pages and an induction of the biblical data, but a deployment of axioms about divine action and human freedom which govern the theological conclusion. Such axioms are important, of course, and, as far as the author is concerned, they are sound theological assumptions which all Christians ought to make. But, arguably, what emerges is a rationalistic treatment of prayer. 'Rationalistic' is a word that has more than one meaning. One standard response to Huw Owen's thought as a whole, over the years that he taught and wrote, was that it was rationalistic in the sense that he maintained the capacity of human reason, unaided by special revelation, to figure out certain truths about God and humankind which then act as a theological or philosophical constraint on what Christians believe and affirm. What is at issue here requires a fuller and more precise statement than we can give it and can be approached from more than one direction. On the one hand, Huw Owen sought to ground his thinking in the fundamental affirmations of the Christian Scriptures. On the other, whatever we say of his thought as a whole, the treatment of petition and intercession in this work certainly appears to have a strong rationalistic hue in this sense: human freedom is given a kind of sacrosanctity which overrides close, detailed and sympathetic discussion of the practices of prayer described in Scripture, this freedom being a rational postulate.[15] I enter my demurral;

readers will judge for themselves, but it may be helpful to couch the issue in terms of theological method, even if a different method does not automatically dictate different conclusions.

That leads to a second point, one which is again connected with 'rationalism'. It is the consistent testimony of Western Christians who go for the first time to the so-called 'Third World', and spend some time there, that prayer becomes a much more real and lively experience than before, petitions and intercessions being directed to God in specific ways of which we have simply lost consciousness in an affluent Western society with certain assumed predictabilities in life. To be sure, we do not need to go outside the West to learn such things, but the sociology of global Christianity today and the experience of such Christians as I have mentioned compels us to attend to Latin American, Asian and sub-Saharan African phenomena, for example, as we wrestle with the question of prayer. Our thinking about miracle and healing needs to be informed by the experience of Christians in other and very different parts of the world. This is not to imply that just one set of conclusions will be dictated by such an investigation. Nor is it to suggest that Huw Owen was not a churchman. He certainly was, taking seriously both his responsibilities as a congregational elder in the Presbyterian Church in Wales and his local preaching. I do not think, however, that he regarded access to the praying experience of the global Church as important for our theological understanding of prayer. Does the ensuing treatment not look rather like that of the Cartesian individual?[16] Perhaps I do him a grave injustice here, but I hope that it is not out of order to raise the question in this context.

The third question pertains to the closing chapter, which has a positive treatment of prayers for the dead as long as they are in purgatory and appears to defend Roman Catholic Mariology, in the course of asking about prayers to Mary as intercessor. Now many readers will have strong religious and theological sensibilities here and those of us who both take a different view from that of the author and regard such differences as serious are surely bound to register that fact. This is not the place to enter into an argument on the matter, but three things should be said in relation to Huw Owen's treatment. Firstly, let not those who dissent from the conclusions simply ignore any arguments that are put forward in their favour. Secondly, let us distinguish between issues rather than blanketing them all together, as many of us are apt to do: the existence of purgatory; the status of Mary; veneration of the saints; prayers for the dead. Thirdly, we need to observe carefully exactly what Huw Owen's conclusions are. Sometimes he straightforwardly advocates a position; sometimes he is saying: 'If this is the position that you hold, then these are the conditions under which you must or must not pray'. Again, I must leave the reader with the work to do but attention to the reference to the existence of Satan at the end of chapter 4 will alert us to the need for careful reading here, even if we conclude that the author is making entirely clear what his commitments are. Having said this, many of us will conclude that this chapter shows Huw Owen ordered tradition, and not just reason, in relation to Scripture, in ways from which we should beg to differ.[17]

Finally I commend this volume for three reasons. Firstly, it introduces us to standards of clarity in expression and precision in reasoning which are all too often lacking in theology. If we disagree with something written here, we need to move carefully along all the lines of the author's argument to find out where we think that it goes wrong. It can be a demanding task in the best possible sense of the term. The reasoning is characteristically tight and verbally economical, never the product of an attempt to be logically clever, but the product of an exceptionally lucid mind and sustained meditation on the subject-matter. When Huw Parri Owen wrote something, it was because he had thought about it at some depth. That is by no means universal practice in theological writing!

Secondly, the author's deep reverence for God, as one who is supremely holy, good and loving, marks the work. Classical theism is sometimes represented as though it removed God far from us. Perhaps it does in some forms and presentations, and its tenets have rightly been subjected to scrutiny for a long time. Yet it need not have that sort of religious effect, and the lively sense of God's love not only backgrounds this book but, the reader may agree, frequently breaks the surface. The same is true of God's holiness. At risk of being needlessly polemical, it may be helpful to indicate a sentence by Clark Pinnock which runs thus: 'To work with a history where the outcomes are predetermined and with creatures that are able to resist him is a challenge and, no doubt, a source of great delight even for God'.[18] Resistance to God is sin and the worst thing in the world: are we to say that God delights in a situation which offers him this challenge? In fairness to Clark Pinnock, he may simply not mean what he says. At any rate, Huw Owen, who also denied such predetermination and affirmed the possibility of resistance, would have been horrified at the suggestion that God might take such a positive attitude to our sin.

This takes us to a final and associated point, but one worth making separately. In our prayers, our innate self-centredness comes out very readily: what we pray for, how we pray, and how frequently and when we do so, all betray an attitude of heart that is egocentric. Has any one of us been free from this? Huw Owen strove to show how God is the proper focus of our prayer and he did so because he held that there is nothing greater than God, who is incomparably great, infinitely worthier than anything created. He was about the last person on earth to bare his soul for the world to see. But it is clear that such a conviction was a matter of experience and not just of the intellect. Consider the following words of his from another work, in light of the debates that surround the traditional Western Christian understanding of hell. 'If there is a Hell it will consist wholly in the soul's final separation from God. This separation is bound to cause inconceivable pain. The condemned sinner would be consumed by a frustration and a despair that fully justify everything that has been imaginatively written concerning the tortures of the damned'.[19] For Huw Parri Owen, the prospect of the loss of communion with God was an unbearable thought. We can guess a little, then, of what the reality of communion with God in prayer must have meant for him.

With the publication of this book, it is my pleasure to thank at least five people for their co-operation in producing it. Bill Reimer and Rob Clements, of Regent Publishing, have welcomed this addition to their list and warmly supported the publication of the manuscript. They have been patient, encouraging and conscientious and I add my thanks to Robert Hand, as well, who was involved in the later stages. I am singularly fortunate to have at my daily disposal the service of our secretary to Faculty, Linda Cameron, who typed up this manuscript and so set the editorial process in motion. Finally, I am immensely grateful to Lynn Quigley, who works as a free-lance editor part of her time, for her initial proof-reading of the typescript on my behalf. Anyone who has worked with her will discover a deeper dimension to the word 'meticulous' than they ever thought it could possess, and will say with hand on heart: 'Any errors which remain are my own'.

PREFACE

My aim in this book is to give a survey of Christian prayer as a whole. Prayer has many elements (such as mental in contrast with vocal prayer or vocal prayer in its petitionary form). Prayer too can be approached from various standpoints (such as a biblical or philosophical one). I shall attempt to cover all elements and to take account of all standpoints. I have chosen the word 'basis' in the title of the book for two reasons. First, I shall devote the substance of the book to those forms of prayer that all Christians have in common. Secondly, although I shall comment on those matters of guidance for the practice of private prayer that are prominent in manuals of devotion, I shall be chiefly concerned with the objective structure and content of prayer together with the theological and philosophical questions that they raise.

The plan of the book is indicated by the chapter headings. In chapter 1 I shall analyse the concept of prayer and give a framework for subsequent discussion. In chapters 2 and 3 I shall examine the main forms of vocal prayer: adoration, thanksgiving, confession, petition and intercession. In chapter 4 I shall offer an exposition of the Lord's Prayer, which is the primary and unifying prayer of Christendom. In chapter 5 I shall deal with the following topics: the relation between prayer and belief, the relation between prayer and religious experience, the language of prayer, the place of feelings (or emotions) in prayer, and difficulties in (or obstacles to) prayer. In chapter 6 I shall examine meditation, contemplation and mystical prayer. I shall conclude with a discussion of prayers offered for and to the dead.

I intend the book for a wide range of readers. I have aimed at satisfying the requirements of those who are, or have been, students or teachers of theology or religious studies. But I also hope that the book will appeal to the large body of people who are prepared to reflect on prayer (as on other topics of Christianity) but who have not received theological or philosophical training. I have avoided an unnecessary use of technical terms. When I have used them I have explained them in the course of examining them.

Over many years I have become indebted to so many prayers and so many writings on prayer that I cannot express the debt adequately. In selecting the prayers and writings to which I refer, I was often aware that I could have chosen others of which some will doubtless occur to my readers. The anthology of prayers I have found most helpful is *The Oxford Book of Prayer*.[1] This contains a large number of ancient and modern, liturgical and private, prayers of every kind representing all the main traditions of the Church.

Unless I state otherwise, my biblical quotations will be taken from the Revised Standard Version.

CHAPTER ONE

THE NATURE OF PRAYER

T his chapter is of an introductory kind. My aim is to give an outline or framework of prayer which I shall fill in subsequently. I shall begin by considering attempts to define prayer. This will lead me to the traditional distinction between vocal and mental prayer. I shall then state and comment on the religious beliefs that are presupposed by Christian prayer. I shall conclude with observations on the role of the Holy Spirit in prayer, the relation between private and public prayer, the bearing of prayer on Christian unity, and the place of prayer in the Christian life as a whole.

'Prayer', like 'religion' of which it is a manifestation, has been defined variously. Yet no definition is wholly satisfactory. Most definitions include some constituents of prayer, but they omit others. Some definitions are too narrow. Others are too wide and so fail to differentiate prayer from other elements in the religious life. The same defects occur in the even more numerous definitions that have been given of religion. I shall consider four among the many definitions of prayer that have been offered.

I shall begin with an ancient definition that has often been repeated (with minor variations). It was given by John of Damascus and runs thus: 'Prayer is either the ascent of the mind to God or the decently beseeching of him'.[1] Prayer includes all this. Yet the mind can 'ascend' to God otherwise than by prayer (for example by the recitation of the creed or the contemplation of nature). Also petition is only one among the vocal forms of prayer. I shall next consider two modern definitions of which the first is too wide and the second too narrow. In the article on prayer contained in *Sacramentum Mundi*, Karl Rahner writes that 'all positive religious acts which are directly and explicitly related, both knowingly and willingly, to God may be called prayer'.[2] This definition is too wide. Thus pronouncing the words of baptism is a religious act, but it is not a prayer (although the service of baptism includes prayers). A definition of prayer that is too narrow is the one given by the *Concise Oxford Dictionary*, which defines prayer as 'a solemn request to God' and the corresponding verb as 'make devout supplication to God'. But (as I noted with reference to John of Damascus) petition or supplication is not the only form of vocal prayer.

Prayer, again, has been defined as 'conversation with God'. This has two points in its favour. First, it is consonant with the petitionary form of prayer where we ask and God answers. Secondly, the Old Testament patriarchs and prophets are vividly represented as conversing with God. Yet here, as elsewhere, biblical language needs to be qualified lest it produce an anthropomorphic view of God that conflicts with statements that the Bible itself makes concerning his transcendent majesty. God and humanity are not equal, as two human persons are when they converse with each other. Therefore the adoration of God as one who is infinitely superior to us takes precedence over petition in theistic prayer. Furthermore, speech, when attributed to God, is a metaphor. God does not have a body by which we can identify his presence or, therefore, a voice by which we can identify his answers to our requests.

Nevertheless, even if a definition of prayer which is both inclusive and precise is not available, we can still be sure in essence, and despite blurred edges, what we are talking about when we talk about prayer. There are many parallels to this in other spheres. We do not need to define a thing conclusively in order to recognise it and talk meaningfully about it. In fact, within Christianity there has always been widespread agreement concerning the forms of religious activity that count as prayer. I shall proceed to give an outline of them.

Anyone who seeks to describe these forms is sooner or later obliged to discuss the traditional distinction between vocal and mental prayer. I shall discuss the distinction now, sooner rather than later, for two reasons. First, the distinction gives us as comprehensive a view of prayer as can be given at this stage. Secondly, my subsequent references to the distinction could be baffling or confusing to the reader if I had not previously elucidated and commented on it.

Vocal prayer (as the adjective indicates) is one that is spoken and that, in being spoken, is addressed to God. There is no difficulty in identifying and understanding this type of prayer. It is the type with which most Christians have been familiar since infancy; and its supremely authoritative example is the Lord's Prayer. In its developed state reflected in public worship it takes the forms of adoration, thanksgiving, confession, petition and intercession. Because all Christians practise this type of prayer we already have a clear-cut and universally acceptable notion of prayer.

Next there is mental prayer. This type of prayer is unspoken; it is wordless; it consists solely in a direction of the mind to God and Christ. This type is neither so clear-cut nor so familiar as the preceding type. It is not so clear-cut because various analyses of it have been given. It is not so familiar because, although in its lower stages (often associated with meditation) it can, with perseverance, be practised by ordinary Christians, in its higher stages (often associated with contemplation) it is practised only by those who are, in the strict sense of the word, mystics.

The contrast between the two types of prayer is lucidly stated by the medieval mystic Walter Hilton in his *The Ladder of Perfection.* Hilton distinguishes between three degrees of prayer. The first degree comprises set forms of vocal prayer that are used either in public worship or in private devotion. The Lord's Prayer is the chief example. The second degree is also vocal, but does not employ set forms. This occurs when a person 'speaks to God as though he were bodily in his presence, using such words as best express his feelings and come to his mind at the time'. But 'the third degree of prayer is in the heart alone; it is without words, and is accompanied by peace and tranquillity of body and soul'. Hilton then says of Christians who are in this state that 'their affections become wholly spiritual, their hearts are continually at prayer, and they can love and praise God without serious hindrance from temptations or worldly thoughts'.[3]

The degrees of prayer that Hilton describes have been stated, in varying ways, by other mystics. They agree that the farther one progresses in the spiritual life, the fewer vocal prayers become until there is no need of them at all.

David Knowles expressed it thus in his account of mystical prayer:

> Prayer is seen as becoming gradually less and less a matter of words or motions of the will and more and more a simple loving attention to God, until this merges into a new realization or experience of the presence of God in the soul, with its accompaniment of a new knowledge and love of God, which do not come from any purely human thought or motion.[4]

Although the distinction between vocal and mental forms of prayer is plain, and although it has been drawn continually, the forms are so closely interrelated that they are inseparable. On the one hand vocal prayer is related to mental prayer in the following ways: (a) Vocal prayer has mental aspects. We must understand the words through which we pray. Beyond such understanding vocal prayer involves an attention to God and an elevation of the mind to him. (b) All prayer implies a non-verbal apprehension or awareness of God's objective reality. (c) Even for the ordinary, non-mystical Christian, vocal prayer can pass into mental prayer of a rudimentary kind. Thus a vocal prayer of adoration can be followed by a period of wordless adoration. (d) Vocal forms of private prayer benefit from being preceded, interspersed, and concluded by periods of silence when we simply recollect that we are in the presence of God. (e) There is an intermediate stage between vocal and mental prayer when a person utters the words of prayer silently. In non-religious matters we all practise 'silent speech'. In fact we are often compelled by our surroundings to offer vocal prayers silently. I shall revert to this point at the end of chapter 5.

On the other hand mental prayer presupposes vocal prayer in these respects. All Christians start from vocal prayer. And no Christian outgrows the need for vocal prayer. However far a Christian progresses in his or her own life of mental prayer, he or she must still participate in the vocal prayers of the Church (especially those offered at the Eucharist). Mental prayer (practised privately) and Liturgical prayer (offered corporately) are complementary. This is well put in *Consider Your Call*, a Benedictine theology of the monastic life:

> Each monk should set aside some convenient period of the day when he can keep a rendezvous with God for silent personal prayer, free from interruption and distraction, apart from the times appointed for the divine office. The two activities will assist each other, for 'liturgy, by its very nature, tends to prolong itself in individual contemplative prayer, and mental prayer in its turn disposes us for, and seeks fulfilment in, liturgical worship.[5]

Throughout this book I shall be concerned, unless I state otherwise, with vocal prayer. I shall deal separately with mental prayer in chapter 6. My reasons for concentrating on vocal prayer are these. This is the form of prayer that all Christians can practise. This, therefore, is the form that is normally designated simply and without qualification 'prayer' so that it is the form examined in *A Dictionary of Christian Spirituality*[6] under the usual headings of adoration, confession, intercession, petition and thanksgiving. This form too is presupposed by mystical experts in mental prayer, not only because this is where they start, but also because this is where they continue as members of the worshipping Church.

Nevertheless, a preoccupation with vocal prayer must not be allowed to blind us to its inseparability from mental prayer in the ways I have indicated. Although words are necessary for communion with God in prayer they can become a barrier to it unless they are accompanied by times of silence when we simply open our hearts to God, listen to him speaking to us, and wait on him for fresh outpourings of his grace. I am thinking chiefly of private prayer. But public worship too can be enriched by periods of silence. Two points at which such periods are appropriate are after the lessons (to let them sink in) and in the intercessions (when members of the congregation can be asked to remember those for whom they have a special obligation to pray).

I shall consider next the religious beliefs that are presupposed by Christian prayer in its vocal form. Such prayer presupposes in the first place the beliefs that Christians share with other theists (mainly Jews and Muslims). The chief among these beliefs are that God is one; that he is a personal reality; that he is omnipotent, omniscient, immutable, and wholly good; that he created the world 'out of nothing' (*ex nihilo*); and that his purpose for us, as creatures he made in his image, is that we should imitate his goodness and so be fit for communion with him. These beliefs are implied by vocal prayer in all its modes. Adoration implies that God is perfect in wisdom, power and goodness; and it is accompanied by a sense of our creaturely dependence on him. This sense dominates thanksgiving. We thank God first for our very existence, and then for all the further blessings that come to us from him. Confession implies that we owe a debt of obedience to God as our holy creator; and that all our sin is, directly or indirectly, against him. Petitionary and intercessory prayer imply that God, being omnipotent, can grant and that, being perfect in love, will grant the requests that we make both for ourselves and for other people.

Our petitions and intercessions must be further governed by a consideration of two other divine properties I have listed. First, there is God's omniscience. Because he is omniscient we must avoid the error of thinking that in prayer we can inform him of facts of which he was previously ignorant. Next there is his immutability. God is immutable first in his nature; he is changeless in his wisdom, power, goodness and love (which is an expression of his goodness). Because God is thus immutable his will for us is immutable in the sense that it is immutably set on our good. Therefore the aim of petitionary prayer is not to bend God's will so that it will conform to our wills, but to bend our wills so that they will conform to his will. Therefore too God will grant us only those things that are in accordance with our good as he sees it. It follows that we are entitled to ask him for something only on the condition and with the qualification that to grant it is in accordance with his will. Yet immutability does not imply predestination. On the contrary it is God's will that we should respond to him in prayer, as in other ways, through an exercise of the free will he has given us. I shall develop these remarks when I discuss petitionary prayer in chapter 3.

Christian prayer is thus shaped by the theistic beliefs that are held, in varying degrees, by many of those who adhere to non-Christian religions or systems of religious philosophy. Yet to the extent that prayer is distinctively Christian it is further shaped by those beliefs that are derived from God's revelation of himself in Christ. The three main beliefs are those that became embodied in the doctrines of the Trinity, the Incarnation, and the Atonement. God, orthodox Christians maintain, exists in the threefold form of Father, Son and Holy Spirit; and in the Son he became man for our salvation. These beliefs add a new dimension to prayer in all its forms. Christians adore God in the mystery of his triunity. They thank him for his great love in becoming man for them in Christ in order to save them from sin and fulfil his purpose for them. Their confession is intensified by their sense of being unworthy of this love, by the awareness of how far they fall short of Christ's obedience to God's will, and by the new assurance of God's forgiveness that Christ brings. The chief object of their petitions and intercessions is that they and others should increasingly receive the new life that the risen Christ makes available to them through the Holy Spirit. Christians can pray to each person of the Trinity who each possesses fully the nature of the one, indivisible, Godhead; but the dominant mode of trinitarian prayer is offered to the Father in the Son and through the Holy Spirit. I shall refer to this mode at various points in the ensuing chapters.

Because of the large area of agreement between Christian and non-Christian theists, Christian prayers are sometimes indistinguishable from non-Christian ones. Yet even then in the Church's worship, Christian prayers are often distinguished by such concluding phrases as 'in the name of Christ our Lord' or 'for Jesus Christ's sake' or 'through Jesus Christ thy Son our Lord'. These phrases imply the following beliefs: (a) Christ is the supreme mediator between God and Man. He is so from the divine side in so far as in him God gave a perfect revelation of himself. He is so from the human side in so far as he offered a perfect response to God. (b) Therefore too Christ is the supreme means whereby we commune with God and experience him. (c) Especially we have access to, communion with, and experience of God as our Father in imitation of and (through the Holy Spirit) participation in, the life of Christ as the Father's incarnate Son. And so, although it is appropriate that we should pray through, or in the name of, Christ as the second person of the Trinity, our usage implies belief in the first and third persons also.

Mental prayer of the kind practised by Christian mystics is governed by the same presupposition as those that govern vocal prayer. Belief in God as the creator is here especially relevant. Many non-Christian mystics (for example, Hindus of a monistic or pantheistic kind) claim to experience an actual identity between their souls and God or the Absolute. Yet Christian mystics who remain faithful to their doctrinal tradition claim only to experience a union of knowledge and love in which God and the soul remain distinct in the relation of creator to created. However much they may feel themselves to be indwelt by God in prayer, they are simultaneously aware of his transcendence. Furthermore, they do not claim that through mental prayer they have access to new truths of Christian revelation that are concealed from the mass of non-mystical believers. They claim only to experience in a new way those beliefs that are accessible to all Christians on the basis of the Scriptures and the teaching of the Church.

There is a further belief that affects the Christian understanding of prayer. This concerns the nature, not of God but of man, although it has theological implications. Throughout the history of the Church it has been held that each human person has a soul which is distinct from the body; that the soul bears God's image; and that it is able to survive the dissolution of the body.[7] Certainly the material realm (that includes human bodies) is not to be despised. God created this realm, as he created souls, to be a reflection of his glory and a means whereby his being can be known. Moreover, each person is a psycho-somatic unity in which, during this present life, the soul needs the body for its self-expression and self-communication. The capacity of matter to be a vehicle for spirit receives special emphasis in Christianity, chiefly in its doctrine of the Incarnation, and its practice of the sacraments. Yet the soul transcends the body. It is through the soul that we know God, love him, and commune with him. And this alone would be sufficient to distinguish us, as those made in the image of God's spirituality, from other forms of terrestrial being.

This pattern characterises the life of prayer. Prayer has materialistic, and in particular corporeal, aspects. It can be aided or impeded by our bodily states. Also it expresses itself through material media. Thus we can adore God through nature or through some product of human craftsmanship. We thank God for his material as well as his spiritual gifts. We bring before him our material as well as our spiritual needs. Nevertheless, in prayer the soul has both an originating and a dominant role. It is through the soul that we pray, vocally as well as mentally, in so far as vocal prayer involves understanding and attention. It is in the soul that prayer becomes a means of activating the divine image in us. Finally (as I shall later have cause to stress), it is principally for spiritual gifts that we ought to pray.

I shall conclude with observations on the four topics that I mentioned in the opening paragraph of this chapter: the role of the Holy Spirit in prayer, the relation between private and public prayer, the bearing of prayer on Christian unity, and the place of prayer in the Christian life as a whole.

1. I have already said that distinctively Christian prayer takes a trinitarian form. I now wish to single out the part played by the Holy Spirit. Here, as in other areas of theology, it is easy to neglect the work of the Holy Spirit so that even if we are nominally trinitarians we in fact become binitarians. In Christian prayer the Holy Spirit is active in these ways. It is he who moves us to pray and who draws us on in the ascent of our minds to God. It is he who enables us to address God as the Father of the Son and who thereby makes us sons of God 'by adoption and grace'. When we pray to the Father or the Son for their

spiritual gifts it is the Holy Spirit who conveys the gifts to us. It is he who, in answer to our prayers, illumines us, strengthens us, and conforms us to Christ by imparting the virtues that Paul enumerates in Galatians 5 where he calls them 'the fruit of the Spirit'. Finally, it is the Holy Spirit who unites Christians within the church as the Body of Christ and who thereby provides the corporate setting of prayer to which I shall refer in my next two comments.

2. Prayer can be either private (when a person prays by himself, alone) or public (when he prays as part of a worshipping congregation). Both types of prayer are sanctioned by the teaching and practice of Jesus. He told his hearers to pray in secret; and he himself spent periods of withdrawal in solitary prayer. But he also attended synagogue services and gave his disciples a prayer for them to recite together. The two types of prayer are complementary. Each enriches the other (as we have already seen in the case of the relation between mental prayer and liturgical prayer). On the one hand, private prayer is likely to wither if a person cuts himself off from the worshipping Church. On the other hand, corporate prayer on Sundays needs to be reinforced by private prayer on weekdays if it is to become a means of spiritual growth. In fact it is impossible to separate the two types of prayer completely. On the one hand in public worship the worshipper must make the prayers his own. On the other hand in praying privately the Christian ought to maintain a sense of belonging to the Church and to offer intercessions for his fellow members of it.

3. Prayer is vitally linked to the fact of Christian unity. Corporate prayer is more obviously linked to it because in public worship we pray together. Yet private prayer is also linked because in this too we ought to recollect our membership in the Church. Prayer (above all the Lord's

Prayer) is itself a sign of Christian unity. It brings together Christians of various denominations. Furthermore, Christians are obliged to pray for unity. We here tend to think primarily, perhaps only, of institutional reunion between different churches. Yet there is a far deeper, spiritual, unity for which we must pray. This is the unity spoken of by Jesus in his 'high-priestly' prayer recorded in John 17. Thus in verse 21 Jesus prays for his disciples 'that they may all be one; even as Thou, Father, art in me and I in Thee, that they also may be in us, so that the world may believe that Thou hast sent me'.

4. Finally, there is the place of prayer in the Christian life as a whole. Here we must maintain a right sense of proportion. On the one hand prayer is only one element in Christianity. Among the other elements there is the whole vast area covered by the attempt to formulate beliefs in the light of scripture, reason and experience. Even within the restricted sphere of public worship prayers form only one element alongside the reading of the scriptures, the preaching of the word, the celebration of the sacraments and the singing of psalms, canticles and hymns. On the other hand prayer is essential to Christianity for these reasons (in addition of course to the purely historical reason constituted by the place occupied by prayer in the Bible and the tradition of the Church).

(i) In terms of form, prayer is a unique way of expressing the personal nature of our relation to God; for in it we address God directly. (ii) In terms of content our relation to God requires us to adore and thank him, to confess our sins to him, and to present our supplications to him. (iii) Prayer is a uniquely effective way of opening our hearts to God and receiving the gifts he bestows on us through the Holy Spirit. (iv) Although we can experience God in many ways, prayer is an especially potent way. In particular prayer brings us close to God; it makes us aware of his presence with us. Within mental prayer this reaches its climax in mystical union. But it occurs also within the vocal prayers offered by ordinary Christians, as a recent writer has observed in a perceptive treatise on Christian spirituality.

> Prayer is not a discipline that will go away from us. If we put it on one side for days or for weeks, sometimes for months or for years, God will not harass us or nag us, nor even hide himself from us. But we will know—like a member of a family knowing that letters, phone calls, even Interflora flowers, are becoming a way of evasion, keeping at a distance what should be seen, held and shared—we will know that there is a closeness to God that will come by prayer and by no other way.[8]

Prayer, therefore, is a unique and irreplaceable part of our response to God. Most obviously it is so in the sense that in it we are responding to him in ways appropriate to his being and self-revelation. In prayer too we are responding to God in ways appropriate to our own nature as creatures who are made in his image and meant for eternal life with him. Prayer is furthermore a response to God's invitation. God desires us to pray in order that by praying we may enter into communion with him and so fulfil his purpose for us. Prayer, therefore, is a wholly natural activity because it is in accordance with the nature of God, the nature of human beings, and the nature of the relation that God wills to establish with us. This does not mean that prayer is always easy. It is often difficult because of our preoccupation with the things of this world. It therefore requires effort and self-discipline. Yet it remains a profoundly natural act that, as such, ought to be marked increasingly by spontaneity and joy.

I shall next examine the main forms of vocal prayer.

Although these must be examined separately they interact as different modes of one activity. I shall begin with adoration.

CHAPTER TWO

FORMS OF VOCAL PRAYER (I): ADORATION, THANKSGIVING, AND CONFESSION

ADORATION

Adoration is defined thus in the *Concise Oxford Dictionary* in terms of the verb 'to adore': 'regard with utmost respect and affection; worship as a deity'. The definition treats 'adoration' as equivalent, in a religious context, to 'worship'. This reflects common usage in which the words occur interchangeably. Nevertheless, adoration is more appropriate in speaking of prayer because, whereas all kinds of prayer occur within the Church's services of public worship, adoration is distinct from other kinds of prayer that are offered both in public worship and in private devotion.

Both 'adoration' and 'worship' can be used with reference to human objects. Thus a lover can say that he adores his beloved and worships the ground on which she treads. Yet these usages are, by comparison with the religious usage, hyperbolical. On further acquaintance the lover may find that his beloved has defects that make her far from adorable. A test of marital love and fidelity is their endurance despite the defects by which the partners are scarred. In any case only God merits adoration to an absolute, unrestricted, degree; for only he is infinitely and immutably perfect in all his properties. In order to mark the difference between God and his creatures here the Church has sometimes distinguished between the adoration (*latreia*) due to God and the veneration (*douleia)* appropriate to the saints. We venerate the saints, not simply for themselves, but for the ways in which they reveal the grace of the God whom alone we adore.

A suitable point of contact between religious and secular usage here is afforded by the concept of 'admiration'. We admire people for their good qualities, actions and achievements even when we recognise that they are defective in other respects. Admiration reaches its unqualified form in our adoration of God. This is stated by Richard Harries thus:

> The capacity to worship is rooted in a person's capacity to admire. This is a capacity shared by believer and non-believer alike. It belongs to our very humanity and all except the psychopath and most hardened cynic display it on occasion. What distinguishes the believer from a person without any religious faith is that he has come to admire something or someone without reserve. He has made a total response to that which he conceives to be of supreme worth.[1]

Adoration is closely linked, not only to worship, but also to praise and wonder. Adoration and praise, like adoration and worship, can be used interchangeably. Thus in addressing God we can say both that we 'adore' and that we 'praise' him for his great glory. Adoration is also closely linked to wonder. A good example is one of F.W.

Faber's well-known hymns, 'My God, how wonderful thou art, thy majesty how bright, how beautiful thy mercy-seat, in depths of burning light. How dread are thine eternal years, O everlasting Lord, by prostrate spirits day and night incessantly adored'.

There are compelling reasons for placing adoration first among the forms of prayer (as it is thus placed both in the *Oxford Book of Prayer* and in *A Dictionary of Christian Spirituality*). First, religion begins and ends, not with us and with our concerns, but with God and with the revelation of himself that he has given us. Prayers of adoration and praise are by nature theocentric. We adore and praise God simply and solely for what he is. Secondly, adoration both determines and outlasts thanksgiving, confession, and petition. It determines them by permeating the spirit in which they are offered and, in particular, helping us to avoid the self-centredness to which our petitions are prone. Adoration outlasts other forms of prayer in so far as when we have offered them it remains as a mental attitude to God. This has an eternal dimension. The ultimate aim of prayer is to prepare us for the life of heaven where, in Charles Wesley's often sung words, we shall be 'lost in wonder, love, and praise'.

The Bible abounds in passages expressing the praise and adoration of God. Within the Old Testament the main source is the Psalter. Some psalms praise God in general terms. Others praise him for his glory and majesty, for his creative power, and for his goodness to Israel. All the last six psalms (145–50) are psalms of praise. The first of these begins, 'I will extol thee my God and King, and bless thy name for ever and ever'. The last is an exuberant exhortation to praise God with musical instruments both for his glorious majesty and for his mighty works. Many passages in the New Testament also express the adoration and praise of God and Christ. In Philippians 2:10–11,

Paul affirms that God exalted Jesus so that 'at the name of Jesus every knee should bow and every tongue confess that Jesus Christ is Lord, to the glory of God the Father'. In Hebrews 13:15 the author says this of Jesus: 'Through him then let us continually offer up a sacrifice of praise to God'. Admittedly not all biblical texts that ascribe praise and glory to God and Christ are explicitly prayers in the strict sense of words addressed to God or Christ; but they are all prayer-like, and they can all be transformed into explicit prayers.

Furthermore, prayers and prayer-like statements of praise occur constantly in the liturgy of the Church. I have already quoted a hymn invoking God as the object of adoration. Here are some other examples. First, there is the recitation of the *Sanctus* at the Eucharist. 'Holy, holy, holy, Lord God of hosts, heaven and earth are full of thy glory. Glory be to thee, O Lord most high'. A splendid hymn directed towards the presence of Christ in the Eucharist is the one by Aquinas beginning *Adoro te devote, latens Deitas.* The first verse, in the standard English translation, runs thus: 'Thee, we adore, O hidden saviour thee, who in thy sacrament doest deign to be: both flesh and spirit at thy presence fail, yet here thy presence we devoutly hail'. Then there is the *Te Deum* which begins as follows: 'We praise thee O God: we acknowledge thee to be the Lord: all the earth doth worship thee, the Father everlasting'. Finally, there is the trinitarian *Gloria* that is used in various contexts (especially after the recitation of psalms).

The point I now wish to emphasise is one I have already stated. This is that adoration is theocentric. We adore, worship and praise God for what he is. According to traditional theism God is infinite in wisdom, power and goodness; he is immutable and eternal; he exists necessarily by the power of his own being; and he created the world 'out of nothing' so that it cannot add anything to his perfection. In all these respects he is, in Anselm's celebrated definition, *id quo nihil maius cogitari potest* (that than which nothing greater can be conceived). As such he evokes our unqualified worship and adoration.

The adoration of God is accompanied by awe, reverence and 'godly fear'. The classical analysis here is the one provided by Rudolf Otto in his *The Idea of the Holy*. For Otto the core of religion consists in a sense of the numinous that he defines as *mysterium tremendum et fascinans*. John Macquarrie sums up the meaning of these terms thus:

> *Mysterium* points to what is called the 'wholly other' character of the numinous Being, which, as suprarational, utterly transcends the grasp of conceptual thought. The element of *tremendum* points to the awe or even the dread experienced in the face of the majesty, overpoweringness, and dynamic energy of the numinous presence. The element of *fascinans* points to the captivating attraction of the numinous being, evoking rapture and love.[2]

The second adjective in this definition (*fascinans*) adds a factor which I have not so far mentioned but to which I shall return shortly.

Adoration, then, is theocentric and disinterested. In adoring God and praising him we turn away from ourselves to the contemplation of his great glory. We do not ask anything for ourselves. Our gaze is fixed wholly on him. Admittedly, when we worship him as the creator we are (as Otto noted) aware of ourselves as his creatures. Yet our attention is still fixed on his creative might. There are here analogies in non-religious experience. The lover, in 'worshipping' and 'adoring' his beloved does so in self-forgetful contemplation of her qualities. The same self-forgetfulness and pure attention to objective reality occur when we wonder at the beauty of nature or admire heroic deeds.

However, a qualification may seem to be required. As the biblical texts I have cited indicate, Christians praise God, not only for himself, but also for the goodness and love he shows to mankind. In so far as we praise God for the blessings he confers on us it may seem that our praise is not disinterested. Yet even here the disinterestedness and objectivity of adoration remain. Our gaze is still fixed, not on the benefits God has bestowed on us, but on the love revealed in the bestowal. In order to have a full understanding of this we must note that the Christian worship and adoration of God are differentiated from non-Christian forms of them by the fact that they are directed towards God as the triunity of Father, Son and Holy Spirit. This is well illustrated by the hymn beginning 'Holy, holy, holy, Lord God almighty'. The particular point of relevance here is that according to the doctrine of the Trinity, God is not merely loving in relation to us; he is so in himself, in the mutual love of the three persons. God's very nature is constituted by this love that, therefore, is the final object of adoration.

There is a further attribute of God that we must consider, especially when we think of his 'attractiveness', the *fascinans* aspect of his being. This is his beauty. We do not hear much of this today. Yet the thought of God's beauty was a major element in Augustine's spirituality. Even if Augustine was here influenced by the Platonic idea of spiritual love (*eros*) for absolute beauty, he adapted Platonism to the Judaeo-Christian understanding of God and of the soul's relation to God. Augustine's instinct was right. If beauty is a valued aspect of finite things and persons it, alongside truth and goodness, must have its archetype in God. And if we are attracted to and admire human persons for their beauty (above all beauty of character) how much more must we be attracted to and adore the infinite beauty of God.

Adoration has two further characteristics. First, it is distinctively offered to God in his transcendence. Admittedly his immanence is also involved in so far as all true worship and prayer are inspired by the Holy Spirit. Moreover, the person who adores may be simultaneously aware of God's indwelling presence and even of the union with God that this presence makes possible. Nevertheless, in offering adoration we are primarily aware of God's transcendence. We are aware of him as one who transcends us in his being as the infinite creator. We are thereby also aware of him as one who far transcends all the positive terms we apply to him. The latter form of transcendence means that the language of adoration is characterised by the *via negativa* whereby, in applying negative terms to God, we exclude from him all the limitations inherent in his creatures.

Secondly, because adoration focuses the mind on the unimaginable nature of God's glory, it is, for the ordinary Christian as well as for the mystic, especially suited to mental prayer. Confession and petition are necessarily verbal. Adoration also can be verbal. The verbal form is the one I have so far been considering. Yet adoration can also be non-verbal. Occasions can arise when we simply adore God in the elevation of the mind to him. This has so often been regarded as the essence of mental prayer. Even when we have finished a verbal prayer of adoration, the mood of adoration can persist. A case can therefore be made out for saying that the concept of adoration is religiously prior to the concept of praise in so far as the latter concept more readily suggests verbal formulation.

Furthermore, in considering the adoration of God offered by the Church we must recollect that 'the Church

23

militant' here below is invisibly one with 'the Church triumphant' above. One reason I gave for assigning priority to adoration among the various forms of prayer was that it has an eternal dimension. Among all the ascriptions of praise to God and Christ that are contained in the New Testament a special place is occupied by those attributed to the celestial hosts in the book of Revelation. Of these the best known runs: 'Worthy is the Lamb who was slain, to receive power and wealth and wisdom and might and honour and glory and blessing'.[3] In adoring Christ on earth we unite ourselves with the far larger body of those who adore him in heaven. Therefore the *Sanctus* at the Eucharist is fittingly introduced with the words: 'With angels and archangels and all the company of heaven, we worship and adore thy glorious name, evermore praising thee and saying "holy, holy, holy"'.

In drawing this account of adoration to a close there is an important qualification I must make. Although the act of adoration directly refers to God and not to ourselves, it is indirectly of benefit to us by helping to free us from the self-concern and self-seeking that separate us from God and prevent us from finding our fulfilment in him. We become most truly ourselves when we are lifted out of ourselves in the worship and praise of God. William Temple put it thus:

> Worship is the submission of all our nature to God. It is the quickening of conscience by his holiness; the opening of mind with his truth; the purification of the imagination by his beauty; the opening of the heart to his love; the surrender of will to his purpose—and all of this gathered up in adoration, the most selfless emotion of which our nature is capable and therefore the chief remedy of that self-centredness which is our original sin and the source of all actual sin.[4]

Lastly, although adoration is distinct from and religiously prior to other forms of prayer, it is closely related to them. It is thus related to confession and petition. The contemplation of God's holiness makes us aware of our sinfulness. It thereby leads us to confess our sins and to ask for God's forgiving grace. The self-abasement that worship entails leads to the submission of oneself to God's will. All this is indicated by Temple when he says in the passage I have quoted that the worship of God is 'the quickening of conscience by his holiness' 'the opening of the heart to his love, and the surrender of will to his purpose'. Adoration is even more closely related to thanksgiving, as these words of the Psalmist show: 'Enter his gates with thanksgiving and his courts with praise'.[5]

Thanksgiving has sometimes been distinguished from adoration on the ground that, whereas we adore God for what he is, we thank him for what he has done. This distinction contains a core of truth. I have more than once affirmed the disinterested nature of adoration which is directed to God himself. But we usually thank God for his goodness toward us that is revealed in his acts of creation and redemption. Yet this contrast is not an absolute one. On the one hand, thanksgiving can be directed to God's being *per se.* Perhaps the best example here is the *Gloria in Excelsis* in which we give thanks to God for his 'great glory'. On the other hand, we praise God as well as thank him for his saving love in Christ. The difference here is one of emphasis. In praising God for his love we contemplate it simply for what it is, 'love so amazing, so divine'. In thanking God for his love we thank him for all those benefits that his love confers on us.

However, although we cannot rigidly separate adoration from thanksgiving with regard to their objects, and although they are intimately connected, they remain distinct. If they were not distinct they would not be

distinguished as they are both in liturgy and in theology.
I shall next discuss thanksgiving.

THANKSGIVING

Just as the Bible contains many prayers or prayer-like
expressions of adoration, so it contains many prayers or
prayer-like expressions of thanksgiving. For the purpose of
illustration let us consider the Pauline epistles. Sometimes
Paul speaks of thanksgiving in general terms. Thus he
says in I Thessalonians 5:17–18: 'Pray constantly, give
thanks in all circumstances', and in Philippians 4:6: 'In
everything by prayer and supplication, with thanksgiving
let your requests be made known to God'. At other times
Paul's references to thanksgiving are specific. Thus in I
Corinthians 15:57 he says this of Christ as the conqueror
of sin and death: 'Thanks be to God, who gives us the
victory through our Lord Jesus Christ'. Elsewhere Paul
thanks God for his fellow Christians and their faith. In
Colossians 3 there are three references to thanksgiving
within three verses (15–17): 'And let the peace of Christ
rule in your hearts, to which indeed you are called in the
one body. And be thankful. Let the word of Christ dwell
in you richly, as you teach and admonish one another
in all wisdom, and as you sing psalms and hymns and
spiritual songs with thankfulness in your hearts to God.
And whatever you do, in word or deed, do everything
in the name of the Lord Jesus, giving thanks to God the
Father through him'.

Among the many prayers of thanksgiving in the
Church's liturgy an outstanding one is the General
Thanksgiving in the Anglican Book of Common Prayer.
This contains the essence of Christian thanksgiving as
well as it can be contained in any one prayer. Although it
will be familiar to some readers, it will not be so to others.

Therefore, because I shall take it as my starting point, I shall quote it in full.

> Almighty God, Father of all mercies, we thine unworthy servants do give thee most humble and hearty thanks for all thy goodness and loving-kindness to us and to all men. We bless thee for our creation, preservation, and all the blessings of this life; but above all for thine inestimable love in the redemption of the world by our Lord Jesus Christ, for the means of grace, and for the hope of glory. And, we beseech thee, give us that due sense of all thy mercies, that our hearts may be unfeignedly thankful, and that we may show forth thy praise, not only with our lips, but in our lives, by giving up ourselves to thy service, and by walking before thee in holiness and righteousness all our days; through Jesus Christ our Lord, to whom with thee and the Holy Ghost be all honour and glory world without end.

This prayer of thanksgiving has three merits. First, it distinguishes between the revelation of God's 'goodness and loving-kindness' in creation and the revelation of them in redemption. Secondly, although it gives verbal priority to the first form of revelation it (again, from a Christian standpoint, rightly) puts the emphasis on the second form. Thirdly, it links thanksgiving to adoration, by its initial use of 'bless', its later use of 'praise', and its final ascription of glory to the Trinity. Lastly, it links thanksgiving to petition in beseeching God to give us such a sense of gratitude to him that we may offer our lives in his service.

A difficulty confronting anyone who sets out to discuss thanksgiving is that it is so comprehensive. It includes everything, directly or indirectly, within its scope. The General Thanksgiving bids us thank God 'for all the blessings of this life'. Yet these are innumerable. Even if we could count them all we could never do justice to the particular ways in which they are bestowed on individuals. I must, therefore, be content with stating them either in general terms or by means of a few examples that I shall leave the reader to supplement from his or her own experience.

Following the order of the General Thanksgiving we must thank God first for his creation of us. It is an axiom of Judaeo-Christian theism that God created the whole world 'out of nothing' (*ex nihilo*). Nothing exists prior to his creative act. This differentiates Christian theology from the view, held in the ancient world by Plato and in the twentieth century by A. N. Whitehead, that God 'creates' by imposing form on pre-existent matter. Furthermore, in creating God does not communicate any part of his substance, any portion of his being, to his creatures. He and they are wholly distinct in their modes of existence. The Christian view of God thus differs from pantheism and panentheism of the kind represented in the ancient world by Stoicism and in the modern world by Hegelianism.

The world is not only *totally* dependent on God in the relation of created to creator. It is also thus *incessantly* dependent on him. A literalistic interpretation of the creation stories in Genesis (as against the symbolical interpretation widely accepted in this century) can easily be taken to support the view that God's creativity was restricted to an initial moment of time, the beginning of the universe, and that afterwards he let the universe continue without his aid. God, however, is the creative ground of the world at every moment of its existence. If he withdrew his creative power it would immediately cease to be. This was affirmed by Augustine through the following analogy. When a builder has finished building a house and departs, the house remains. But the universe would pass away at once if God deserted it. If, therefore, we distinguish (as the General Thanksgiving does) between our 'creation' and our 'preservation' we must take 'preservation' to signify the continuance of the creative act by which we were brought into being originally.

Our fundamental gratitude to God, then, must be for the sheer fact that we exist at all at this and every other moment of our existence. This gratitude ought to become all the greater through the realisation that God does not need us. He is self-existent and self-sufficient within his infinite life of love as Father, Son and Holy Spirit. He created us through an overflowing of the love that is the governing principle of his inner life.

Even to mention, not to say describe, all God's gifts to us by creation is an almost impossible task. We can, however, broadly distinguish between material gifts and spiritual ones, provided we remember that they coalesce in the psycho-somatic unity that constitutes a human person. We must thank God for the whole realm of material nature, not least for our bodies that have their own beauty and are necessary for our spiritual modes of self-expression and self-communication. Yet we must thank God chiefly for our souls. We thank him in the first place and in general for our capacities of thought, imagination, and love. We thank him next for all the particular blessings (special to each one of us) that the actualisation of these faculties confers. Above all we thank God that in our souls he has made us in his image and destined us for eternal life with him.

Beyond all the gifts that God confers on us by creation there is the gift of salvation that he confers on us in Christ. Therefore, in the General Thanksgiving, having thanked God for his created gifts, we proceed to thank him 'above all for thine inestimable love in the redemption of the world by our Lord Jesus Christ for the means of grace and for the hope of glory'. These words, if suitably expanded, contain everything in Christian revelation for which our thanks are due. Obviously I cannot offer such an expansion here. To do so would entail an independent examination of such doctrines as those of the Incarnation, the Atonement, and eternal life. There are, however, two elements in the Thanksgiving's summary which require emphasis. The first is the concept of 'love'. In whatever way we interpret Christ's redemptive work (or, alternatively, whatever view of the Atonement we hold) we must remember that the basis of redemption and atonement, and so the primary object of thanksgiving, is God's 'inestimable love' in becoming man for our salvation. 'God so loved the world that he gave his only Son, that whoever believes in him should not perish but have eternal life'.[6]

Next there is the Thanksgiving's expression 'means of grace'. Among the many means a special place is occupied by the Eucharist (that, in the Greek, means literally 'a giving of thanks'). At the Eucharist, with its recollection of the Last Supper, we thank God principally for the redemptive power of Christ's death. But we ought to thank God also for Christ's preceding life and for his succeeding resurrection, exaltation, and gift of the Holy Spirit. All are interacting phases in a single ministry that, taken as a whole, accomplished all that was necessary from God's side for the salvation of humankind. In a Eucharistic liturgy such a prayer of thanksgiving ought to be inserted at some point immediately before the act of communion. Also afterwards there ought to be a prayer of thanksgiving for the sacrament that has been received.

Furthermore, Christians are obliged to give thanks for the Church, the Body of Christ, and thereby for all its past and present members to whom they are, directly or indirectly, indebted for their faith. Hence services of public worship ought regularly to contain prayers of thanksgiving for 'the faithful and blessed departed'.

Among the special services held in a church or chapel some of the most moving are services of thanksgiving for Christians who testified to Christ by the quality of their lives. But beyond remembering departed souls Christians ought to cultivate a sense of gratitude for the total tradition they have inherited within the community of the Church.

The grounds and the ways I have described prayers of thanksgiving are straightforward. It remains only for us to offer them. However, a problem remains. I shall introduce it by quoting two texts from the epistles of the New Testament. In I Thessalonians 5:18 Paul says, *'In everything (en panti)* give thanks'. This is paraphrased by the RSV, 'In all circumstances' and by the NEB, 'Whatever happens', but in Ephesians 5:20 we are told to give thanks *'for* all things' *(hyper pantōn)*. I shall begin with the second of these texts because this poses the problem. I shall turn later to the first text that points the way to a solution.

It is surely impossible for us to thank God 'for' everything, at least directly and without qualification. Some things that happen to us are desirable and good, but others are undesirable and evil; and whereas we can thank God directly and without qualification for the former, we cannot thus thank him for the latter. Let us consider the case of a married couple who, after years of waiting, procreate a baby who grows into a healthy and attractive child. The couple can wholeheartedly thank God for their mutual love and for the gift of the child. Let us suppose further that at the age of ten the child is killed in a road accident. It is preposterous to suggest that the parents could thank God for this. Many other examples could be given.

Yet Christians can always thank God 'in' all things (or circumstances). In adversity they can remember the blessings that still remain and that are unaffected by the evil event or situation for which they cannot give thanks. They can give thanks too for factors that help to mitigate the pain or grief that the event or situation produces. Thus in my example the parents can thank God for the comfort and strength that they give to each other. In the course of time they may also find themselves able to thank God for the memory of their child. Again, they may come to see and be thankful that good has come out of evil (perhaps by drawing them closer together or giving them a new sense of values).

However, the chief, unsurpassable, ground for gratitude, and one that covers all circumstances, is constituted by the facts that God himself endured wholly unmerited suffering in the person of Christ; that Christ, through his resurrection, overcame both sin and death; and that through the Holy Spirit he enables believers to share his victory. As Paul put it, in words I quoted earlier, 'Thanks be to God who gives us the victory through our Lord Jesus Christ'. This enabled Paul to say, 'We know that in everything God works for good with those who love him, who are called according to his purpose'.[7] Admittedly Christian faith does not miraculously remove the bewilderment and pain that evil causes; but it enables us to endure them in thankful reliance on the grace that Christ offers.

To conclude, I suggest that we often fail to see the necessity of thanksgiving in our lives as a whole. Apart from religion, we owe far more than we can state to other people for all they have done for us and mean to us. Yet we are often lacking in gratitude to them; we so easily take them for granted. Even when we are grateful at the time for an unmerited or unexpected act of kindness our sense of gratitude often quickly disappears. How much more ought we to cultivate a sense of gratitude to God.

I shall next discuss prayer in the form of confession. Confession is doubly related to thanksgiving. Ingratitude is one of the sins we must confess, and God's forgiveness of our sins is one of the chief gifts for which we must thank him.

CONFESSION

Confession is an essential constituent of prayer. Throughout our lives as Christians, despite our access to the sanctifying power of the Holy Spirit, we remain sinners. This is a perennial Christian experience that is reflected in the liturgy of the Church and the testimony of its spiritual writers. It is, moreover, based on the New Testament. Jesus included a petition for forgiveness in the prayer he gave to his disciples; and the moral defects of Paul's converts are evident from his epistles. The author of I John summed it up as follows: 'If we say we have no sin we deceive ourselves and the truth is not in us. If we confess our sins he is faithful and just, and will forgive our sins and cleanse us from all unrighteousness'.[8]

Confession can be either public or private. When it occurs in the public worship of the Church it may be offered either by all the worshippers together or by the minister on their behalf. Private confession also can take one of two forms. A person may offer it to God directly or he may offer it to a priest. I shall consider the first form. I shall not deal with the second partly because it is not practised by a vast number of Christians and partly because it is not strictly a form of prayer.

A verbal confession alone is not enough. In order to be religiously valid and effective it must take place within the context of repentance. If we regard confession as an

33

element in repentance, then it must be accompanied by the other elements of contrition and a resolve to change one's life (in particular to cultivate the virtues and perform the good acts that are opposite to the vices and sinful acts we have confessed). To these elements in repentance we must add a readiness to make amends (where this is possible) to others for the wrong we have done them. Confession too implies trust in God for the forgiveness of our sins. I shall examine the concept of forgiveness in discussing the Lord's Prayer.

Confession can vary in the degrees of its generality (or, therefore, particularity). There is no inflexible rule for determining how general or how particular a confession should be. On the whole a general confession is more appropriate to public worship whereas confession of particular sins is more appropriate to private prayer. However, there is room in public worship for the enumeration of particular sins. Conversely a brief general confession may be sufficient in private prayer. It may even be required for reasons I shall give later.

Unless I state otherwise, I shall have in mind private confession (although much that I shall say will also be applicable to public confession). The details of private confession vary endlessly according to the differences between individuals and their circumstances. I can only suggest the following as some among the principles that ought to govern our understanding of confession and of the self-examination by which it is preceded.

1. In self-examination and confession we must include both the sins of the spirit and the sins of the flesh. There used to be a tendency among some Christians to concentrate on sins of the flesh while not paying sufficient attention to sins of the spirit. Yet the sins of the spirit are apt to be more pervasive than sins of the flesh in the following respects. Whereas a sin of the flesh is often

an isolated and rare occurrence, a sin of the spirit is more likely to corrupt, if not the whole of life, then large stretches of it. One spiritual sin—pride—has been held to lie at the root of all sin and so to define sin's essential character. This view is correct if 'pride' is understood, not merely as 'conceit', but as a radical 'turning in' on oneself and one's own desires instead of 'turning outward' in love for God and one's neighbour. Moreover, whereas sins of the flesh involve sins of the spirit in so far as they imply a misdirection of the self and a corruption of the will, a sin of the spirit need not imply or express itself in a sin of the flesh.

However, we must avoid falling into the opposite extreme of regarding sins of the flesh as being comparatively unimportant. Particularly in reacting against the once prevalent concentration on sexual vice (sometimes to the extent of identifying sin, or at least immorality, with it) we must not think that Christians are permitted to regard such vice as a minor offence that can be easily overlooked. The Judaeo-Christian emphasis on man's psycho-somatic nature means that we are called on to present our whole lives as 'a living sacrifice' to God. We cannot even say that in all cases a sin of the spirit is more serious than a sin of the flesh. Thus a mild feeling of envy by a man who is not normally an envious person is surely not more serious than persistent adultery. Also (as this example suggests), a sin of the flesh can exceed a sin of the spirit in its harmful effect on other people.

2. It is necessary to confess sins of omission as well as sins of commission. In fact the Anglican General Confession places the first before the second. 'We have left undone those things which we ought to have done; and we have done those things which we ought not to have done'. We are inclined to think that sins of omission are less serious than sins of commission. Yet the first type

of sin can be as serious as or even more serious than the second. Thus a failure to visit a sick or bereaved person (*qua* a failure to perform an act of charity) can be as serious as or more serious than an outburst of temper. I suspect that the older we grow the more likely it becomes that our sins of omission will be more numerous than our sins of commission.

3. In self-examination and confession it is necessary to include one's inner life as well as one's outer acts. In fact all sins of the spirit are parts of one's inner life; they are states or activities of the soul even when they are not expressed in external behaviour. Even when we have not 'done' anything that is wrong, we may have thought and desired what is wrong. Our souls can be corrupted by vices even when we do not perform vicious acts. Again, we may perform an act that would otherwise be good but is not so because it is performed with the wrong motive or intention. The importance of inner purity was stressed by Jesus in the Sermon on the Mount. Paul even envisaged the possibility of giving one's body to be burned and yet lacking charity.[9]

4. Christians are especially bound to confess their failure to perform, or their defects in performing, distinctively religious acts. The chief among these acts are attendance at church and the offering of private prayer.

5. We must constantly remember the religious dimension of sin in two ways. First, all our sins are, indirectly, if not directly, against God; for all signify a failure to obey his law, a rejection of his love, and a rupture of the personal relationship that he wills to establish with us. This was normatively expressed thus in the greatest of penitential Psalms: 'Against thee, thee only, have I sinned, and done that which is evil in thy sight'.[10] Secondly, the Christian must judge him or herself, not in the light of purely human ideals of good or decent behaviour, but in

the light of the spiritual and moral perfection commanded and exemplified by Christ and later described in the Epistles. As Christians we are called to be perfect, in our own finite mode of being, as God is perfect, by our co-operation with his grace in Christ.

6. It follows that, although we must confess particular sins of which we are aware, we must go beyond them to discover the extent to which they reflect an habitual self-centredness that is opposed to the self-denial enjoined by Christ and expressed by Paul in terms of 'dying with' Christ in order to 'rise with' him to newness of life. Going with this there is the necessity to discover how far we have allowed ourselves to be dominated by worldliness (by which I mean both an acceptance of worldly values and a tendency to seek our final good in this world rather than in God and in the eternal life that union with him confers).

This, then, is the essence of prayer in the form of confession. Reflection on it raises four further questions. These would need to be given extensive treatment in other contexts. The scope and limits of this book compel me to deal with them briefly. The questions are the distinction between original sin and actual sin, the fact of free will, the question of 'grading' sin, and the question of corporate responsibility.

(a) There is the distinction between original sin and actual sin. According to a usage that goes far back in the history of the Church, original sin signifies the sinful tendencies that all members of the human race inherit from Adam, whereas actual sin signifies a sin committed by a free act of a person's will. On the former it seems to me clear that, although the derivation of human sinfulness from the 'fall' of a supposed first man, Adam, is untenable for the reasons usually given, the empirical facts all indicate that we belong to a fallen race in the sense that, however sin arose, we inherit sinful tendencies that are exacerbated by our environment. Our innate sinfulness is not to be interpreted solely in moral terms that an agnostic can endorse. It consists basically in an aversion and alienation from God whereby we seek our good in ourselves and other creatures instead of in him. We should further note that the fact of original sin (at least in its purely moral manifestations) has been affirmed by philosophers as well as theologians; and that Christians have held, as a matter of experience and not merely of dogma, that they are marred by a corruption from which they are freed by the sanctifying grace of Christ.

In principle the distinction between original and actual sin is plain. In principle too it is (or at least it seems to me) plain that although we must confess our innate sinfulness (our part in 'original' sin) in the sense of acknowledging it and our need of redemption from it, we can meaningfully ask God's forgiveness only for 'actual' sins (that is, those sins that we have deliberately committed through free acts of will). In practice, however, the two forms of sin are so closely linked that a thoroughgoing attempt to separate them in confession must seem artificial, if not impossible. We are so often responsible for not resisting our evil tendencies and for not submitting ourselves to God's help in overcoming them. Our culpable failure in these respects then produces a hardening and extension of original sin.

(b) Actual sin implies the reality of free will. Unless we could have acted differently in the same circumstances we could not be responsible for our sin; and so we should not be guilty of it; and so we should not have occasion to confess it with a view to receiving God's forgiveness. In terms of original sin this means that we must be capable of resisting our sinful impulses if our failure to resist them is to be a valid cause of a confession leading to a plea for forgiveness. The resistance is twofold. First, we do not consent to the impulses by dwelling on them, allowing them to dominate us, and forming intentions under their influence. Secondly, when it comes to the point, we do not act in accordance with them. We must also be capable of freely choosing to invoke God's help if we are to be responsible for and guilty of not invoking it in moments of temptation. There are many arguments for and against free will. My own view is that although the arguments against determinism are very strong, the defence of free will rests ultimately on experience. We simply know, in very many cases, that when we have acted wrongly we could have acted otherwise. We know it immediately. But a test we can often apply is to compare such cases with other similar ones where we have, perhaps after a prolonged struggle, resisted sinful inclinations.

(c) I turn now to the question whether it is possible to 'grade' sins and, if it is so, whether it is necessary or desirable to do so in, or before, confession. A well-known way of grading sins is by distinguishing between 'mortal' sin and 'venial' sin. This distinction cannot be regarded as essential to the Christian concept of sin (and so to confession) in view of the facts that it can be variously interpreted, has been widely rejected by Protestants, and is treated with suspicion by some Roman Catholic theologians. Nevertheless, I must say a few words about it if only because of its place in the moral theology of the Western Church. Mortal sin has been authoritatively defined thus:

> According to Catholic teaching, mortal sin consists in a deliberate act of turning away from God as man's last end by seeking his satisfaction in a creature. This frustration of God's purpose is held to involve the loss of sanctifying grace and eternal damnation. A sin in order to be mortal must be committed with

39

a clear knowledge of its guilt and with full consent of
the will, and must concern a grave matter. [11]

'Mortal sin' as thus defined is full of difficulties. Here
are some. All involve further distinctions (in addition to
the initial distinction between mortal and venial sin).
First, if the 'turning away' from God is complete and
irrevocable it is bound to entail 'the loss of sanctifying
grace and eternal damnation'. In that case confession and
absolution are impossible. Therefore, we must envisage
an incomplete and revocable 'turning away' that does
not carry this entailment and permits forgiveness after
confession. Secondly, we must distinguish between a state
of sin that entails only a partial loss of sanctifying grace
(and so only tends to damnation) and a state of sin that
involves a total loss with consequent damnation. Thirdly,
we are still left to determine what is and what is not 'a
grave matter'.

Nevertheless, it is often possible to distinguish
between sins in terms of their gravity although there
is room for differences of opinion between Christians
in applying the distinction to particular cases. Thus it
seems to me obvious that although it is wrong to speak
irritably even when there is a good reason for irritation, it
is much less wrong than telling a lie in order to advance
one's career. Again, it seems to me obvious that there
are increasing degrees of gravity in experiencing a sinful
impulse, dwelling on it, forming an intention under its
influence, and putting the intention into practice. Is it,
then, desirable to distinguish between more or less grave
sins in private confession? Obviously there would be
something very artificial in applying the distinction, in
every case. Yet it can sometimes be necessary to apply
it either, on the one hand, to make ourselves fully aware
of the more grave sins we have committed or, on the

other hand, to prevent an over-sensitive conscience from becoming obsessed with comparatively minor sins. At the same time we must reckon with these possibilities. What seems to be a more or less grave sin to us may not seem so to God. Also, a less grave sin, if indulgently treated, may foster the tendency towards a more grave one.

(d) There is the question of 'corporate' guilt and responsibility (considered from a moral and religious, not a legal, point of view). Admittedly we ascribe sinful actions to people as members of a group and to the group as a whole. Some of the worst evils are perpetrated by groups, from gangs of criminals to political parties. Even the Church has sinned corporately. Admittedly too many people consent to evils committed by groups to which they belong although they would not commit these evils individually. Nevertheless, although people must acknowledge with regret and shame the total sin committed by a group to which they belong, they can be responsible for and guilty of only their own share in this sin through their own action (or inaction). This share, therefore, must form the content of their confession.

Finally, all our confessions are apt to be defective. Sometimes we may not be sure whether something we have done is sinful and so a cause of confession. If it is sinful and if we ought to have known this we are guilty of not knowing. We are also sometimes guilty of self-deception in the following ways. While recognising that something we have done is normally sinful we may invalidly offer excuses to ourselves for holding that in our case it is not sinful. Yet again, we sometimes fail to uncover our wrong motives or intentions that vitiate acts which would otherwise be good. Even if these defects in our confession are not present we cannot be sure that we have fully confessed all our sins. We may have omitted some either through inadvertence or, more seriously, because we have buried the memory of them by relegating them to our unconscious or sub-conscious minds (from which, of course, they may later arise to haunt us). Furthermore, concentration on particular sins can conceal from us the sinful states that these sins express. It can conceal our persistent self-centredness and self-seeking, our persistent failure thereby to love God and our neighbour as ourselves, and our persistent worldliness. None of us can measure the extent to which we are thus marred at the deepest level of the soul. And few of us are not here guilty of an evasion or a self-deception that can be caused by the fear of exposing ourselves fully to the burning light of God.

Two consequences follow for our prayers of confession and the petitions by which they are accompanied. First, although we must examine ourselves for our particular acts of wrongdoing, our awareness of possible defects in our confession requires us to make a general confession of all that has been and still is wrong in our lives and that is known only to God. Secondly, we must ask God to forgive us for all culpable defects in our confession no less than we must ask him to forgive those sins that we explicitly confess.

CHAPTER THREE

FORMS OF VOCAL PRAYER (II): PETITION AND INTERCESSION

F ollowing common linguistic usage I shall take petition to signify requests for oneself and intercession to signify requests for, or on behalf of, other people. However, although the two are distinct they are closely related so that to a large extent they raise the same questions and are subject to the same religious principles. Therefore much that I shall say about petition will be applicable to intercession also. I shall sometimes point out the application although it would be tedious to do so in every case. I shall begin by examining petition. I shall then deal separately with problems raised by intercession but not by petition.

We must approach petition (and, no less, intercession) with a due sense of proportion. On the one hand we must resist the tendency to equate prayer with petition or even to regard the petitionary form of prayer as the dominant one. Petition is subordinate to adoration and thanksgiving. Prayer begins and ends with the adoration of God and with thanks to him for all his gifts. On the other hand it would be wrong to regard the petitionary form of prayer as a low grade one that we outgrow when we reach spiritual maturity. To do so would be contrary to the place that petitions occupy in the New Testament (chiefly in the Lord's Prayer). Moreover, thanksgiving and confession lead to petition. Thanksgiving leads to it in so far as we ask for God's grace that we may show our thanks, not only with our lips, but also in our lives. Confession leads us to ask God for his forgiveness and sanctifying power.

The petitionary and intercessory forms of prayer are the ones that are most apt to cause difficulty for reflective people. Once we grant the existence of an infinitely perfect creator who out of love became man for our salvation, few questions are raised (or problems constituted) by adoration, thanksgiving and confession. Admittedly, the first and, especially, the second of these may sometimes seem hard to sustain when they are put in the context of evil (especially evil in the form of innocent suffering); but evil is the chief difficulty for theistic faith in all its aspects; and it cannot be discussed adequately as an interlude in a book devoted to prayer. Petition and intercession, however, raise many questions and problems that I shall discuss.

A true understanding of petitionary prayer must rest on the recognition of two ways in which petitions addressed to God differ from petitions addressed to human beings. First, we cannot inform God of anything he does not already know. Secondly, we cannot change his mind and will. These facts are stated by Aquinas thus:

> Petition is different when addressed to men and when addressed to God. With human intercession we seek to inform another person of our wants, and then to sway his will on our behalf, but neither of these considerations applies when we pour out our prayers to God.[1]

The first point of difference is obvious in one respect. In asking a human person for something we often simultaneously inform him of something of which he was previously ignorant. Thus when a child asks his father for a particular toy at Christmas, the father may not have known previously that the toy existed or, therefore, that the child desired it. Or (to take a more profound analogy and one that is closer to intercession) someone collecting for Christian Aid may request a contribution from a person who was previously ignorant both of the charitable enterprise and of the particular purpose (such as the relief of a famine-struck area) for which the collection was being made. These forms of ignorance cannot apply to God. We cannot inform him of anything he does not already know. Having created the world *ex nihilo* he is necessarily omniscient; he has a complete knowledge both of external facts and of our desires with regard to them.

There is also another sense in which our requests to God differ from our requests to each other here. God does not merely have a perfect knowledge of our wishes and circumstances; he also has a perfect vision of our good. What we desire may not be for our good as God sees it. Again, even if it is good for us it may conflict with some good that God wills to confer on someone else. Therefore, God, having a perfect vision of what is for his human creatures' good, must refuse to grant our petitions if they conflict with this good. Certainly human persons too sometimes refuse to grant requests because to grant them would be contrary to the good of a person or persons. Thus a father may rightly refuse to give a child something the child wants because to give it would be contrary to either the good of the child or the good of the family as a whole. Yet there is no human parallel to God's capacity to know completely what is for each person's good when this is viewed both in relation to other people's good and *sub specie eternitatis.*

This brings us to the second way in which our requests to God differ from our requests to other human beings. In making requests of a human person we often do so, as Aquinas puts it, 'to sway his will on our behalf'. But we cannot sway God or change the will of God. We cannot persuade him to act more wisely or more generously toward us, for his wisdom and generosity are infinite and unvarying. To think that we can change God's will by our petitions runs counter to the sense of creaturely dependence on him that animates our prayers of adoration, thanksgiving and confession. Moreover, to think this can easily lead us to believe that we can manipulate God so that he will satisfy all our desires, however trivial or self-centred they may be.

The ultimate aim of petitionary prayer should be, not to conform God's will to our wills, but to conform our wills to his will. This was affirmed by Aquinas thus later in the passage from which I have quoted. 'For our sake is prayer necessary, that we should consider our needs and bend our desire fervently and devoutly to receive what God wishes us to have so that we may become worthy to receive his blessings'. Therefore all our petitions, especially those offered for the occurrence of particular events, must be accompanied by the qualification, 'If it is in accordance with thy will'.

Here a discussion of the New Testament is required, if only to avert misunderstanding. According to the Sermon on the Mount Jesus says, 'Ask, and it will be given you'.[2] Later in Matthew's Gospel he is recorded as saying, 'Whatever you ask in prayer, you will receive, if you have faith'.[3] If these promises are taken without qualification they affirm that God will grant all our requests, whatever they may be. However, the promises must be interpreted in the light of other sayings attributed to Jesus in the Synoptic Gospels. First, in the Sermon on the Mount Jesus proceeds to affirm, by way of analogy, that if we, evil as we are, bestow good gifts on our children, how much more will God bestow good gifts on those who ask him.[4] This implies that God will bestow only 'good' gifts; and this must mean gifts that are good in his sight. If a human father refuses to give his child something the child requests because he considers that this would not be good for the child, how much more will our heavenly Father refuse to grant us gifts that in his eyes are not for our good.

The chief synoptic evidence for the necessity of qualifying our petitions is the prayer that Jesus himself offered on the eve of his passion: 'Abba, Father, all things are possible to thee; remove this cup from me; yet not what I will, but what thou wilt'.[5] If, at the supreme crisis of his life, Jesus, the perfect Son of God, qualified a petition in a matter of life or death, how much more ought we sinners to qualify our petitions by asking God to grant us something only if it is in accordance with his will. In fact, Jesus' petition was not granted. He died cruelly and shamefully in order to give a final revelation of God's saving will.

We must further note the qualifications of petitionary prayer contained in the fourth Gospel that here, as elsewhere (especially in Christology), supplements the Synoptic Gospels by giving them a further degree of interpretation. In John 14:13–14 Jesus is represented as saying this: 'Whatever you ask in my name, I will do it, that the Father may be glorified in the Son; if you ask anything in my name I will do it.' In the next chapter Jesus promises, 'If you abide in me, and my words abide in you, ask whatever you will, and it shall be done for you'.[6] Similar statements occur in the first Epistle of John. The author writes that we receive from God 'whatever we ask, because we keep his commandments and do what pleases him', and that if we ask anything according to the will of Christ he hears us.[7]

Our requests, then, will be granted if (and only if) we make them in the name of Christ and according to his will, if we abide in him, and if we keep God's commandments. Three things must be noted concerning these Johannine qualifications. First, there is no conflict between asking for something according to God's will and asking for it according to Christ's will; for Christ perfectly expressed God's will both divinely by incarnating God's will of love and humanly by his obedience to that will. Secondly, we must think not only of the earthly Jesus but also of the exalted Christ. We are to pray as Christ now wishes us to pray. Thirdly, we cannot pray according to the will of Christ unless we abide in him and keep God's commandments.

The principles governing petitionary prayer that I have examined are stated, with characteristic cogency, by William Temple as follows in his *Readings in St. John's Gospel* in an appendix devoted to Christ's teaching on prayer.

> First, must be put the fundamental principle that God is perfect love and wisdom; he has no need that we should tell him of our wants or desires; he knows what is for our good better than we do ourselves, and it is always his will to give it. Consequently we must not in prayer have any thought of suggesting to God what was not already in his mind—still less of changing his mind or purpose.

A little later, after quoting relevant verses in the fourth Gospel, Temple concludes thus:

> This means that the essential act of prayer is not the bending of God's will to ours—of course not—but

the bending of our wills to his. The proper outline
of a Christian's prayer is not, 'Please do for me what
I want', but, 'Please do in me, with me and through
me what you want'.[8]

However, an important question arises here. From
the beginning Christians have attached causal efficacy
to prayer. They have believed that God grants us things
because we have asked for them. This is reflected in their
descriptions of prayer. Thus when a prayer is answered
they say that it has been 'efficacious'. I shall later argue
that while some prayers can have causal efficacy, others
cannot have it. But my purpose now is to qualify the word
'because' and the phrase 'causal efficacy'. God grants us
things because we have asked for them only because he has
willed so to grant them. This was made clear by Aquinas
when he wrote, 'We do not pray in order to change the
decree of divine providence, but in order to impetrate
those things which God has determined will be obtained
through our prayers'.[9] The commentator in the Blackfriars
edition of the text observes that Cajetan, a leading
interpreter of Aquinas, 'describes prayer as an efficient
dispositive cause for obtaining the thing requested'. It is
an efficient cause only in so far as it disposes us to receive
what God wills to give us in response to our prayers. And
it may be his will not to give what we ask for. There is here
a large difference between the requests we make of God
and the requests we make of each other. The latter requests
often have causal efficacy in the sense of changing the
will of the person of whom we make the request either
by informing him of facts of which he was ignorant, or
by persuading him to act favourably either towards us or
towards other people.

A consideration of God's will is specially pressing
in relation to requests for material benefits or for the

occurrence (or non-occurrence) of events. Before or after we make such requests we must place them in the light of God's will in the following two ways. First, before making the request we must ask ourselves whether it is in accordance with our understanding of God's will. Is this the sort of thing for which we ought to ask God? Alternatively, is this the sort of thing that we can validly expect God to grant us? Examination of the request may compel us to answer negatively or at least to experience grave doubt for many reasons of which these are some. The request, if not wrong *per se*, may be wrongly motivated. Or it may reveal a reprehensible preoccupation with prestige or power or comfort or success or material wealth. Secondly, even when a request is in accordance with our understanding of God's will, it may not be his will to grant it. Therefore we must qualify the request with the words 'if it is in accordance with thy will'. We must do so both in the imitation of Christ and in view of the extent to which God's vision of our good transcends our understanding.

Yet it may be said that there are some requests of a religious and moral kind which we can be sure are always in accordance with God's will so that there is no need for them to be qualified. In a general sense this is true. The testimony of scripture entitles us to be sure that it is God's will to grant us all that is necessary for our salvation. It is his will to forgive our sins, to sanctify us by the Holy Spirit, and to grant us an eternal life formed by loving union with him. This is the merest outline of the spiritual gifts that God is ready to bestow on us in answer to our prayers. In principle, therefore, we can say, as a fundamental affirmation of Christian confidence and hope, that it is God's will to grant us those petitions that stem directly from the revelation of himself and of human destiny that he has given us in Christ.

However, when we move from the general to the particular it by no means follows that God will grant all our spiritual and religious requests. A petition for a spiritual gift may rest on religious misunderstanding. Within the New Testament an acute illustration is the request made by James and John that they may sit alongside Jesus in his glory. To this Jesus makes the following reply: 'You do not know what you are asking. Are you able to drink the cup that I drink, or to be baptised with the baptism with which I am baptised'? When the two disciples answer that they are able Jesus says this: 'The cup that I drink you will drink; and with the baptism with which I am baptised you will be baptised; but to sit at my right hand or at my left is not mine to grant, but it is for those for whom it has been prepared'.[10] Also, a spiritual request may be selfishly motivated. The request made by James and John was of this kind in so far as (to quote Temple again) 'it was for something which by gaining they would keep others out of it'. Even a prayer for sanctity may have a self-centred motive. A person may seek sanctity as his own possession and as a form of self-glorification, that produces in him the smugness and 'holier than thou' attitude that are so objectionable and that Jesus condemned in the Pharisees.

Again, we may find a spiritual request not granted because, although what we ask for is desirable and good, God has his own reason for not granting it in this case. Thus a minister or priest may pray for an increase in the size of his congregation. His prayer may be selfishly motivated; he may be moved by envy of those among his fellow ministers who have larger congregations, or he may wish to gain a reputation for pastoral 'success'. Yet let us suppose that this is not so and that he is motivated by evangelical zeal. He may still not find his prayer granted. It may be God's will that he should thereby learn, or learn afresh, that the worth of his ministry, and the spiritual vitality of his flock are not amenable to quantitative assessment.

Yet again we may find that a spiritual request is not granted in the manner we expected and desired. Let us consider a prayer for the acquisition of a virtue or the eradication of a vice. There can be no doubt that God will grant the prayer by the gift of his sanctifying grace. But he will do so in his own time and his own way. It would be wrong for us to expect that God will create, or increase, a virtue instantly, completely, and irrevocably so that we are exempt from all future inclination to the contrary vice and thereby from the need to practise the virtue by opposing the inclination through the exercise of our free will. We may even find that occasions soon arise when the practice of the virtue is tested with special severity. Thus we may find that a prayer for patience or chastity is immediately followed by a situation in which, although we are aided by divine grace, we still need an effort to resist impatience or lust.

These, then, are the basic principles of petitionary prayer. I shall conclude this section with an objection. It has been argued that because God knows what is for our good and is willing to grant it, there is no need for us to make requests of him. This objection can be answered in these ways which show that petitionary prayer is not merely consonant with, but demanded by, the personal nature of our relationship to God. (a) Jesus taught us to think of our relation to God by analogy with the relation of children to their earthly fathers. Now, if a child finds it natural to ask his or her father for good things, it is natural that we should ask God for them. (b) We owe everything to God as our creator. Asking him for his gifts is an appropriate way of expressing this debt. (c) Petition is a special way of entering into communion with God and experiencing him. (d) More particularly petitionary prayer is a special way of opening our hearts to God and disposing ourselves to receive his gifts. Here it is important to recognise that, so far as our prayers for spiritual gifts are concerned, it is impossible to draw a rigid line of demarcation between asking and receiving. D. Z. Phillips made this point with reference to two examples: a request for deeper faith and a request for overcoming envy.

> One cannot distinguish here between the asking for and the receiving, as one can between the asking for and the receiving of a loan. To ask God for something in the above examples is already to have begun receiving. To ask in prayer to overcome a weakness is to begin overcoming it. In certain prayers, then, such as prayers for deeper faith and devotion, a request made to God is the beginning of God's answer.[11]

A major question now arises. Can all petitions and intercessions possess causal efficacy in the sense that God grants us or other people things because we have asked for them (as a human father bestows gifts on his children because they have asked for them)? Obviously God will grant us only those things that are religiously and morally good, and only if to grant them is in accordance with his will. But if these conditions are met are we entitled to expect that all our petitions and intercessions can be causally effective? Or are there some cases in which we have good reason for not expecting this? In answering these questions we must make two distinctions. We must distinguish between prayers for spiritual gifts and prayers that are either for material gifts or for the occurrence (or non-occurrence) of events. We must also distinguish, where this is necessary, between petitions (prayers for oneself) and intercession (prayers for other people).

Before I proceed there are some matters of principle I must clarify. I shall maintain that there are grounds for holding that while some petitions and intercessions can, others cannot, possess causal efficacy in the sense I have given. In other words, although there are grounds for expecting God to do some things in response to prayer (provided the prayer satisfies the appropriate religious and moral criteria), there are also grounds for not expecting him to do other things in response to prayer (even when the prayer satisfies these criteria). To this it may be objected that we have no right to place restrictions on the power of prayer, still less on the power of God himself. My reply is as follows. First, we all distinguish between those things that we can and those that we cannot appropriately ask God to give us in response to our prayers. Thus while all Christians would regard it as proper to ask God for the increase of a moral virtue, few, if any, Christians would regard it as proper to ask God for the gift of intellectual talents in which they are by nature wholly lacking. The question is not whether but where we draw the distinction. Secondly, quite apart from prayer, Christians modify the idea of God's omnipotence by distinguishing between the things that God can do and the things that he cannot do because to do them would be contrary to his nature or to the nature of the world that he created.

Yet the fallibility of the human intellect, the differences of opinion that here exist among Christians, and the element of mystery inherent in God's relation to the world make it improper for us to claim finality and incorrigibility for the limits that we place on the causal efficacy of prayer. All I claim is to give reasons why in my opinion it is doubtful whether we can validly ascribe causal efficacy to some kinds of prayer. The reasons are partly negative and partly positive. They are negative in so far as in some cases I simply cannot see how, or in what manner, God could act in answer to prayer. The reasons are positive in so far as in other cases, in my view, there are grounds for supposing that he could not thus act. However, in the negative cases there may be ways that are humanly comprehensible but that I have failed to comprehend, in which God could act in answer to these prayers. Or he may answer them in ways that are known to him alone. In the positive cases it is possible that the grounds I give for not attributing causal efficacy to the prayers in question are invalid and that such prayers can be causally effective either in ways which are humanly comprehensible but which I have not comprehended or in ways known to God alone. Ultimately, therefore, I am agnostic and preserve an open mind.

My last principle is of a practical kind. It is one thing to distinguish, as an act of objective reasoning, between prayers that do and prayers that do not have causal efficacy; it is another thing to observe the distinction in a matter of life and death where our own feelings are involved. Thus when someone is overcome by anxiety for a loved one whose life is in danger it is likely that he will pray for the loved one's deliverance even if he holds, in moments of detached reflection, that there are reasons for thinking that the prayer is of a kind that cannot be causally effective. On this I offer the following observations. (a) Provided the person has ultimately left (as I leave) the question of the prayer's efficacy an open one, he does not fall into self-contradiction; for in offering the prayer he is desperately hoping that the prayer can be effective in some way he has not been able to comprehend. (b) The prayer will be acceptable to God on account of the faith that it expresses. (c) Both those who do and those who do not think that a prayer can be causally effective coincide in so far as both must qualify the prayer with the words 'if it is in accordance with thy will'.

On the basis of these principles, then, I shall consider the question of prayer's causal efficacy first with reference to petitions for spiritual gifts. As I noted in chapter 1, these petitions must be given primacy. The primary goal of the Christian is to be united through the Holy Spirit with the Son in the Son's self-offering to the Father. It is for this union and the spiritual transformation it entails that the Christian must primarily pray. Certainly Christians must not disparage the material world which God has created to reflect his glory and to which they belong as psycho-somatic beings. Also Christians must not be indifferent to worldly events over which God rules with his providential care. In prayer we must bring before God our material as well as our spiritual needs. We must also bring before him those worldly events that are rightly the object of our concern. In fact, spiritual petitions include asking God for the illumination and power to act in the world and cause worldly events in accordance with his will. Nevertheless, the primacy of the spiritual remains.

This primacy is reflected in the New Testament. The petitions and intercessions contained in the latter are of a predominantly spiritual kind. The chief example is the Lord's Prayer. Nearly all its petitions are spiritual. The only exception is the petition for our daily bread; and some exegetes have given even this a spiritual interpretation.[12] Admittedly, the New Testament elsewhere states or implies prayers for material blessings. Also, it includes prayers for both the occurrence and the non-occurrence of events.[13] Yet even these prayers are often placed in a spiritual context or given a spiritual qualification.[14] The primacy of prayers for spiritual gifts is also affirmed in the Old Testament.[15] The same primacy is present in the forms of liturgy used by the Church. In these the main emphasis falls on petitions for forgiveness and for grace to persevere in the Christian life. Finally, mystical prayer is governed by a desire, not for this or that material good or state of affairs, but for union with God in Christ.

There is no difficulty in positing a causal connection between our petitions for spiritual gifts and God's granting of them. It is wholly in accordance with the personal nature of God's relation to us that in answer to our prayers he should grant us those spiritual gifts that are necessary for our salvation. There is therefore no difficulty in supposing that he indirectly causes physical states and outward occurrences in answering such petitions. Thus if he grants us patience we shall inevitably show patience in our bodily behaviour and external acts. In fact, we often pray for virtues in a particular situation in relation to particular people and with particular actions in view. The total effects for good of all the petitions for spiritual gifts offered by Christians throughout the ages is incalculable.

However, a verbal distinction is needed here. I have deliberately spoken of 'petitions for spiritual gifts', not simply 'spiritual petitions'. Not all the latter can have causal force (or at least have it directly and without qualification). Let us take the two petitions in the Lord's Prayer 'thy kingdom come' and 'thy will be done'. These cannot be causally effective as they stand; they cannot bring into being or in any way affect God's kingly rule and sovereign will. Yet the petitions become causally effective when we refer them to ourselves and take them to mean 'may thy kingdom come in me' and 'may thy will be done by me'; for they then imply the further petition that we may be given grace to accept God's reign and to do his will in our lives.

Assuming, then, that prayers for spiritual gifts can possess causal efficacy, I suggest that difficulties arise over attributing such efficacy to prayers of the following kinds: (i) both petitions and intercessions for events that fall wholly within physical nature and that are therefore subject to scientific investigation, (ii) petitions either for people to act in particular ways or for the occurrence of events other than those specified under (i), (iii) petitions for material objects or (in a commonly used sense of the word) 'things', (iv) intercessions for the spiritual good of other people, and (v) intercessions involving requests for the occurrence of events that are caused by other people. I shall proceed to examine (i), (ii) and (iii). I shall examine (iv) and (v) when I consider intercession separately.

I shall, then, first examine prayers for the occurrence of events that fall wholly within physical nature and that are therefore subject to scientific investigation. (I am now excluding miracles but I shall refer to them later.) The difficulty is to see how such prayers could make a difference or (to express the same point in other words) how God could grant our requests simply and solely because we have made them. If events are determined by those laws which God has imparted to nature and which science investigates it is hard, and for me impossible, to see how the events could simultaneously occur as answers to our prayers. Let us consider the matter in terms of causality. How can an event be caused both by a preceding event and by our petitions? In so far as nature proceeds according to its own dynamism and exhibits its own patterns of behaviour it leaves no room for influence by prayer. Thus a physical disease either is or is not curable in terms of the patient's physical state and the medical treatment available. Again, the climatic conditions are such that rain either will or will not fall in a particular area. How, then, can prayer affect either the cure of the disease or the advent of rain?

Admittedly there is one sphere in which there is *limited* scope for God to act in an *in*direct and *mediated* way on nature. This is disease to the extent that mental factors operate. Some diseases are of a psycho-somatic kind. The physical symptoms are partly or wholly caused by mental factors. Even in the case of a purely physical illness a patient's recovery can be helped or hindered by his mental state. If, then, we believe that prayer can causally affect our mental states or the mental states of other people we can believe also that prayer can thereby affect the course of a disease. However, to the extent (which is often very large and sometimes total) that a disease and its methods of treatment are of a purely physical kind and are beyond mental control they are outside the scope of causally effective prayer.

There are, so far as I can see, two ways of attempting to justify the attribution of causal efficacy to prayers for purely physical events. I hold that both are invalid. First, there is the view that at the microcosmic level studied by atomic physics nature is subject to an element of indeterminacy and chance which leaves scope for God to act in response to prayer. However, even if such indeterminacy exists, it is still true that at the macrocosmic level accessible to our normal powers of perception uniform and predictable sequences occur that enable us to formulate countless propositions of the kind 'if X occurs, Y follows'. Thus one writer who holds this view admits that microcosmic chance often becomes macrocosmic necessity.[16] Secondly, there is the view propounded by H. H. Farmer in chapter ten of his *The World and God*. Farmer offers the following grounds for maintaining both that in response to prayer God initiates events which would not otherwise occur and that these events are susceptible to scientific explanation. In its inner, invisible, reality nature consists in entities (comparable to Leibnizian monads) that exhibit primitive forms of mentality which are open to such new effects as God chooses to produce in them but which lie outside the sphere of scientific investigation. However, the postulation of such entities is highly speculative and wholly unverifiable. In any case it must again be said that on the outer and visible level investigated by science nature is characterised by regular sequences that Farmer himself describes as a 'fixed order' and even 'mechanical necessities'.[17]

It may be said in reply that we human beings produce effects in nature which would not occur without our agency, yet which are in accordance with the laws of nature; and that *a fortiori* such effects can be produced by God in answer to our prayers. It is true that we can produce such effects. Indeed, our temporal welfare depends largely on our capacity to produce them. Here are two among the many examples that can be given. First, through the administration of a drug, a doctor can effect a cure that would not otherwise occur. Again, through the sowing of seed a gardener can produce a plant that would not otherwise be produced. Yet to ask God to cause such effects is to ask him either (a) to influence human beings so that they will cause the effects, or (b) to cause the effects in place of human agents. (a) is ruled out by the fact that I am now considering prayers for God to act on nature directly, not indirectly through human agents; (b) is ruled out by the fact that we should then be asking God to perform a miracle (in the first case by causing a drug to appear unaided in the person's body, and in the second case by causing seed to appear unaided in the soil).

I therefore conclude that the only way in which God could answer a request for a purely physical event is by performing a miracle. 'Miracle' has been variously defined. I offer the following definition as one that accords with traditional usage and posits the greatest degree of contrast between the miraculous and the non-miraculous. A miracle is 'an unusual event of a physical or material kind that supersedes the laws of nature and is due to a supernatural act of God'. The concept of the miraculous raises many questions, but only one concerns us now. Can we expect God to work miracles? It is surely clear that we cannot expect him to do so either in answer to prayer or of his own volition. God normally governs nature through the laws with which he has endowed it. Although he is the primary cause of everything he normally acts in the material realm through secondary causes which he allows to operate without any intervention on his part. Therefore, although we may feel driven to ask God for a miracle we cannot expect him to perform one. If he decides to perform one his decision is necessarily unpredictable. It is for our good that God rarely performs miracles. If he were to perform them frequently, nature would not have the uniformity and predictability that enable us to understand it, control it for our use, and plan our lives according to our expectation of its future states.

In earlier times many Christians were able to think in terms of causally effective petitions for physical events because they regarded God as having already intervened in nature for some special purpose. This was particularly the case with regard to their prayers for God to remove physical states of an adverse kind (such as famine, drought and plagues). They viewed these states as divinely imposed penalties for sin. Their prayers, therefore, were acts of confession which they hoped would cause God to remove the penalty. However, for a long time the majority of reflective Christians have rejected this view of divine punishment on the grounds that it is contrary to the universality of the laws governing nature's operations; that it implies a false conception of God's moral government of the world; and that it is not confirmed by the facts. Thus with reference to the last ground, it would be absurd and morally repulsive to suppose that Ethiopian peasants are afflicted by famine as a punishment for being especially wicked. If any people deserve punishment they are those who support the warring factions by which the effects of the famine are increased.

Furthermore, causally interpreted prayers for purely physical events or states are exposed to the following dangers. First, we seek to locate God's actions in the 'gaps' left in scientific accounts of the natural world. Apart from those who appeal to the indeterminacy of nature at the microcosmic level, there are some who attempt to find a place for divine responses to prayer in macrocosmic areas where our understanding of nature is incomplete and our capacity to predict its future states is inexact. But such gaps in scientific knowledge may one day be closed so that no scope for a non-miraculous act of God will remain. A second danger is that we view material states which we take to be answers to prayer as 'observable differences' whereby God's activity, and so his existence, are verified. But this exposes belief in God to the possibility of falsification, as an experiment made by Francis Galton at the end of the nineteenth century shows. Galton claimed to invalidate petitionary prayer by a statistical appeal to empirical evidence. He found no evidence for holding that sick people who prayed or were prayed for were more likely than others to recover or to recover rapidly. A third type of danger also concerns prayers for the recovery of the sick, but it concerns them in a different way. Belief in the causal efficacy of such prayers can cruelly raise false expectations. It can also obscure the fact that there is always a large number of people who are terminally ill; and it can divert us from our obligation to care for them. The fourth type of danger affects all prayers for physical states or observable occurrences. Such prayers can easily become trivial or self-centred. Even when they are not so they can blind us to the primacy of spiritual petitions. This is especially relevant to prayers for the gravely sick. We must all die. Our final prayer should be that we so endure our mortal afflictions that we may be fit for eternal life with God.

However, even if our petitions do not causally affect physical events we can still validly offer many of them. There is one that all Christians are obliged to offer. This is the petition for our daily bread in the Lord's Prayer. (Bread, of course, does not come to us from nature ready made; it needs to be made by human hands. But so far as its constituents are due to natural processes it falls within the category of petition I am now examining.) Jesus commands us to offer this petition although, in the same sermon, he affirms God's universal and undiscriminating providence when he says that God 'makes his sun rise on the evil and on the good, and sends rain on the just and the unjust'. Later Jesus forbids anxiety about food and drink on the grounds that God knows we need them. If, nevertheless, Jesus commands us to pray for our daily bread we can invoke his authority for other similar prayers (such as those for the physically sick or for seed-time and harvest without which bread could not be produced).

The reason why we can validly offer such prayers is one I have already given in defence of petitionary prayer as a whole. The reason is that to ask God for his gifts is one way in which we acknowledge our dependence on him and avert the danger of taking his gifts for granted. Even if a petition is not causally effective it can still function in this way. In both causal and non-causal types of petition, the same fact of absolute dependence on God that prompts us to thank him for his past and present gifts prompts us also to ask him for his future gifts which are a continuation of his past and present ones. Thus our prayers for our daily bread or for the physically sick are religiously inevitable ways of expressing our dependence on God for the continuation of those natural processes whereby bread is produced and the sick are healed.

Therefore, Christians find it entirely natural to pray for physical events that fall within the sequence of cause and effect that scientists investigate. From a theological standpoint such investigation does no more than provide further understanding of God's universal providence that Jesus affirmed.

Difficulties further arise over ascribing causal efficacy to petitions either for persons to act in particular ways or for the occurrence of events other than those that occur wholly within physical nature and that I have already examined. These two types of petition can coincide when the events are caused by other people. Reflection prompts two questions here. What are we asking God for when we offer such petitions? And can we validly expect God to act in the modes that our petitions state or imply? I shall illustrate these questions by some examples.

My first example is taken from John Baillie's Gifford Lectures.[18] Baillie recalls from his youth a man who prayed that a girl with whom he had fallen in love would respond to his love and consent to marry him. He then made this into a religious test. If God refused his request he would renounce his faith. In fact the girl rejected him. Baillie rightly observes that such a test of God is outrageous. But it also seems to me that the initial request is questionable. What exactly did the man expect God to do? How did he expect God to act? Baillie writes that the man 'used to pray fervently that the girl might be led to respond to his love'. But how was she to be 'led' and how could God affect the 'leading'? The only answer I can think of is that God himself should lead her to reciprocate her suitor's love and to accept his offer of marriage. Yet how could God thus lead her? So far as I can see he could do so only by causing her to change her emotions as well, perhaps, as causing her to ignore good reasons she had for not marrying her suitor. Yet could her suitor have validly expected God to exert such influence? To put it in a general form, can we validly expect God to change people's feelings, attitudes, and choices without their conscious, rational, and free co-operation? I do not think so. It is, I hold, contrary to God's personal relation to us to suppose that he would act on persons in this way at all, and especially that he would do so in order to fulfil another person's wish.

Here are two other examples. Let us consider the case of a man who is about to sit an examination. He prays that he may pass. How does he expect God to act? Surely he does not expect God to help him to answer the questions by supplying him with information he did not previously possess. Surely, again, he does not expect God to influence the examiners in his favour. Such expectations would be contrary to justice; for the man would in fact (if not in intention) be asking God to act in ways that would involve injustice to the other examinee. *Mutatis mutandis* the same difficulties are raised by the case of someone who prays that he may obtain a post for which he will shortly be interviewed. Prayer is indirectly relevant to the events mentioned in these two examples. Thus in preparing himself for an examination a person can validly ask God for the gift of perseverance – a gift for which he can validly ask God in many other contexts. Again, a person can validly ask God for grace to seek God's will in the outcome of an interview. But such prayers are very different from prayers based on the hope that in answer to them God will act in ways ensuring that the person praying will pass the examination or be appointed to the post.

Finally there are petitions or requests for material objects or 'things'. Thus a person may pray for a new house, a television set, a car. The propriety of such petitions can be plausibly queried on the ground that they reveal a preoccupation with material possessions that is contrary to the teaching of Jesus. This, however, is not now my concern which is to raise the same questions which I raised with regard to the preceding types of petition. What are people who make such requests expecting God to do? How do they expect him to act? What they want is enough money to buy the house, the television set, the car; so that in effect they are asking God to provide the money. How, then, do they expect him to provide it? These questions would remain even if a person prayed for material things, not for himself, but for other people.

As the end of the preceding paragraph indicates, the difficulties in the petitions I have been examining are also present if we reformulate the petitions as intercessions (that is, if we pray that other persons should marry, pass an examination, or obtain a post). I shall next discuss intercessory prayer as such. In the course of the discussion I shall consider afresh prayers requesting God to act on other people.

Many of my preceding remarks on petitions apply also to intercessions. I shall now consider intercessions separately. I shall start with the commonly held view that intercessions can be causally effective in the sense that in response to them God acts in ways in which he would not otherwise have acted. I hold that this view is questionable in two areas: our prayers for the spiritual welfare of other people, and our prayers for the occurrence (or non-occurrence) of events that depend on decisions taken by other people.

Let us, then, examine prayers for the spiritual welfare of, or for the granting of spiritual gifts to, other people. I shall first consider the following objection to the causal interpretation of such prayers. If this interpretation were correct, God would put our welfare to that extent in each other's hands; and people who were prayed for would enjoy an advantage over those who were not prayed for. I think that this objection is sound. It has sometimes been replied that in other ways God places our spiritual welfare in each other's hands. We are constantly influencing each other for good or bad. This reply is true so far as it goes. Yet it is inadequate in these respects. Although we are subject to bad influences as well as good ones, God has given us free will whereby we can accept the good influences and reject the bad ones. Secondly, it would, I submit, be contrary to both God's justice and his love if our salvation depended on the prayers of other people, even if these prayers did no more than tilt the balance in our favour.

However, I do not wish to press this objection. The chief difficulty, and the only one on which I want to rest my case, is that it is hard to see how our intercessions can affect God's attitudes to, or actions on, other people. God knows the needs of us all and is constantly seeking our good. There is here a special need for us to avoid supposing that we can inform God of things or persuade him to act more favourably toward us. We can so easily frame our intercessions in such a way that we fall into thinking that we can bring the needs of the world to God's notice or (so to speak) give him a 'push' so that he will show an extra degree of interest in, or care for, those for whom we pray. Here human analogies can be misleading. One person often intercedes for another in the hope of causing a change of mind in a third person. Thus a father may plead with his son's employer to show mercy to his son when the latter has committed an offence meriting dismissal; and he may reinforce his plea by urging an extenuating circumstance (such as some strain to which his son has been subject). But God knows all our circumstances, and his mercy is unvarying.

Yet (it may be said) does not the same objection apply to spiritual petitions? If God is omnipotent, omniscient and infinitely loving is it not also inappropriate for me to expect that he will bestow spiritual gifts on me because I ask him? The answer is a negative one for reasons I have given. In asking God for spiritual gifts for myself, I am not (if I am praying rightly) informing him of my needs or asking him to be more generous to me. Rather the petitionary form of prayer is a way of expressing my dependence on him, placing myself at his disposal, and being receptive to his gifts. But each person must do this for himself. I cannot do it on behalf of someone else.

The second problem concerns prayers for the occurrence or non-occurrence of events that depend on decisions taken by other people. Here we are, implicitly if not explicitly, asking God to influence people so that they will make the decisions that will produce the results we desire. But God could not influence them without either making them different persons or infringing the free will with which he has endowed them. An example of the first influence would be if God granted to a person a form or degree of ability that the person did not previously possess. The most obvious example of the second influence would be if, when a person is faced with a choice, God impelled him to choose one course of action rather than another. The two types of influence can co-exist (as would be the case if God were to increase a person's moral goodness without any free effort on the person's part or any free co-operation with God's grace).

Let us consider prayers for the peace of the world where the actions of many people (chiefly the leaders of nations) are involved. I shall illustrate this from recent history. Before the Gulf War broke out at the beginning of 1991, many prayers for peace were offered. But the choice between peace and war rested with Saddam Hussein. It was up to him to comply or not to comply with United Nations resolutions and withdraw from Kuwait. Were we praying that God would suddenly change the heart of

68

Saddam so that he became a new man who renounced all thoughts of aggression and desired only justice and peace? Or, on the assumption that he remained a cruel tyrant, were we asking God to obliterate his freedom of choice by so manipulating his character, motives and intentions that he would be compelled to withdraw? On a much larger scale, and if we substitute 'Hitler' for 'Saddam', the same things could be said, in principle, of prayers for peace offered before the outbreak of the Second World War in 1939.

So far I have been considering intercessions in the strictly theological and properly religious sense of asking God to act on or for others. Yet some people have given the impression of thinking that intercessions have causal efficacy in their own right. A few years ago the Archbishop of Canterbury's special envoy Terry Waite was, to widespread rejoicing, released from captivity. Among the published letters attributing his release to prayers offered on his behalf some implied that the prayers themselves were causally effective apart from any action on the part of God. One letter went so far as to speak of a great 'wave' of prayer that influenced Waite's captors. Such a view of prayer is, I maintain, untenable for these reasons. First, the idea of a causally effective psychic energy that affects people's dispositions and actions over long distances has no basis in what we otherwise know of the scope of our mental powers. Secondly, belief in such an energy would not be equivalent to the belief that God himself acts on and through other people in response to our intercessions. And it is the latter belief which is my subject now.

Nevertheless, even if we do not consider our intercessions to be causally effective in the sense that in response to them God acts on or through other people, we can still validly offer them. We can do so because they are wholly natural ways of expressing our concern for others to God, just as non-causally interpreted petitions are wholly natural ways of expressing our dependence on him. We can put it yet more strongly. Just as there is no substitute for petitions, so there is none for intercessions. There is no comparable way of bringing the needs of the world before God. The test of this is that if we were to drop intercessions and retain only petitions we should feel, rightly, that our prayers were marred by the very self-centredness from which we must pray to be delivered (or, alternatively and positively, that our prayers lacked the charity which is one of the chief gifts for which we ought to pray). To this we must add the testimony of scripture and tradition to prayers of intercession. To jettison them is unthinkable.

I suggest that our intercessions should be governed by two principles. The first is one that I have just indicated. In all things we ought to aim at pleasing God. We please him most by showing love (or charity) towards each other. Intercession is the way in which we express our charity through prayer. Secondly, remembering that the ultimate aim of petitionary prayer is obedience to and union with the will of God, we should regard our intercessions as ways by which we identify ourselves with God's will for other people and, thereby, with the hidden ways in which he ceaselessly seeks their good. These principles have three corollaries. (a) We must pray primarily for the spiritual good of other people. (b) It is sufficient for us to cast our intercessions in a general form. We can safely leave the particularisation to divine providence. (c) We shall often find it also sufficient to state our intercessions in terms of 'remembering' the world's needs before God or 'committing' people to his care. These terms are often used interchangeably in worship. Thus the minister may begin with the words 'let us present our intercessions to God'. He may then continue 'let us remember the victims of conflict in former Yugoslavia' or 'let us commit the sick to God' (when members of the congregation may be named).

Furthermore, even if we exclude a causal connection between our intercessions and God's actions, we can still see how in other ways intercession makes a difference both to the intercessor and to those for whom he intercedes. First, there is the intercessor. Through intercession we see people, not in relation to ourselves and to the ways in which they satisfy our needs, but as they are in themselves, creatures who exist in their own right and who are the objects of God's love. This perception of them increases our sensitivity to their uniqueness as individuals, their circumstances, and their claims upon us. And this new sensitivity leads to action. Thus a husband cannot pray truly for his wife without renewing his resolve to act considerately towards her. Also just as intercession is inseparable from action, so it is inseparable from petitions for discernment and power to help those for whom we intercede. It is therefore appropriate that an anthology entitled *Prayer in a Troubled World*[19] should contain petitions as well as intercessions. Intercession can also make a difference to the person for whom it is offered. It does so indirectly by prompting charitable action towards the person. It does so directly in so far as a person can be comforted and strengthened by the knowledge that prayers are offered for him by his fellow Christians. I can think of many examples within my own experience.

There is yet another way, following from what I have said, in which intercession is causally effective. Intercession is often discussed in general terms without reference to its setting in the Church. But this setting is crucial for intercession of a distinctively Christian kind. To the extent that we are Christians we intercede for each other as fellow members of Christ's body. Both for the one who prays and for the one who is prayed for intercession increases our awareness of our unity in Christ. In the first place this occurs when a local congregation intercedes for those of its number who are in distress. This can then develop into, if it is not already accompanied by, a sense of our fellowship with the Church universal.

My conclusion, therefore, is that, with the exception of the very rare cases in which God grants requests for a miracle, only petitions for spiritual gifts have causal efficacy. However, when we bear in mind that many petitions and intercessions can be offered non-causally, that intercessions have causal efficacy on the human plane, and that the external effects of spiritual gifts are enormous, we can see that there is plenty of room for prayer in its petitionary and intercessory forms. Furthermore, even if we extend the scope of causally effective prayer beyond the limits I have set we must still acknowledge the following fact. From a Christian standpoint what primarily matters is not whether this or that event (due either to physical processes or to human agency) occurs or does not occur. What primarily matters is that in all occurrences we should seek to do God's will. Therefore, in either success or failure, self-fulfilment or frustration, health or sickness, our final prayer should be for the guidance and strength of the Holy Spirit.

In the light of my preceding discussion I shall next offer some observations on, first, God's answers to our prayers and, secondly, the fact of unanswered prayer. The idea of God's answers to our prayers can be taken in either a strong or a weak sense. According to the strong sense God answers our prayers when he grants us something because we have asked for it so that there is a causal connection between the request and its fulfilment. According to the weak sense God is said to answer our prayers when what we ask for coincides with his providential ordering of nature (as when our prayer for our daily bread is answered by the continued operation of those physical laws that enable bread to be produced). I shall adopt the strong, the causal, sense for these reasons. (a) This is the sense that we normally give to the idea of God answering prayer. (b) This too is the sense we normally have in mind when we speak of answering the requests we make of each other. Thus if I write to a friend asking him to grant me something, and if he has already offered me that thing in a letter that has crossed mine in the post, I do not find it natural to say that he has granted my request although the request has been fulfilled. (c) It is the strong, causal, sense that creates difficulties (especially in the negative form of unanswered prayers).

The point I now wish to make is that it is impossible to prove by an appeal to external evidence that something is God's answer to a prayer. There is here again a difference between answers to requests we address to God and answers to requests we address to human persons. In many human cases we can be sure that something is an answer to a request because there is an observable connection between them. This connection is forged partly by spatio-temporal location and partly by speech. Thus if a son asks his father for a gift, if the father promises to bestow it, and if the gift follows the next day, it would be straining scepticism absurdly to doubt a causal connection between the request and the gift. Yet God is not a visible entity acting within a spatio-temporal setting; and he does not verbally converse with us. Hence his answers to our requests are not amenable to the forms of verification that are applicable to the requests we make of each other.

Nevertheless, if a Christian prays for a spiritual gift and if the gift is granted he has good reasons for believing that the granting is due to the prayer. Here we must note again that to ask God for spiritual gifts is already to begin to receive them. This unity of asking and receiving that the believer experiences makes it inconceivable (at any rate for him) that the relation between them is coincidental. We have to take account further of the facts that in the Christian life there is a developing sequence of occasions on which God's answer to prayer is a felt reality; and that beyond the particular gifts he confers on us in response to our prayers there is a general sense of his presence that he increasingly imparts to us in the course of this conferment.

Yet attention is normally focussed on *un*answered prayer when our requests have not been granted. This has often been regarded as a problem. I shall suggest (what may seem surprising to the reader) that there is no problem. (By this I mean that there is no problem for theology. Of course from a practical point of view the acceptance of unanswered prayer is often hard.) We do not see a problem in the fact that many of the requests we make of each other are not granted. We recognise that there may be many reasons why a request has been refused. I suspect that people often see a problem in God's refusal of our requests because they assume that the aim of petitionary prayer is to obtain from God whatever we want. But on the assumption that a problem does exist I shall begin by rejecting two ways of solving it.

First, it has been said that when a prayer has been unanswered in the sense that the request we made has not been granted God has in fact answered the prayer by giving the answer 'No'. But the fact that he has said 'No', not 'Yes', is the so-called problem. Secondly, it has been said that God sometimes answers prayer, not directly by granting what we asked for, but indirectly by granting us something else that may be better for us. An example I have seen given is of a pilgrim to Lourdes who, while not receiving the prayed for cure obtains new faith and joy through a deeper sense of his fellowship with other Christians. Peter Baelz put the point as follows:

> If I claim that God had in a way answered my prayer by refusing to grant my petition, I am not necessarily wriggling out of a difficulty, but I am saying that in and through his refusal I have apprehended something more of his presence and activity. The answer in this case is in terms of a deeper religious awareness, of a growth in a personal relationship with God.[20]

This is profoundly true. But what we should say is, not that a prayer has been differently answered, but that God's refusal to answer it has ministered to our good in other ways.

I suggest, then, that unanswered prayer is not a problem. There are many reasons why God does not always answer prayer. First, if my earlier account of petitions and intercessions is correct, some prayers are unanswered because by their nature (and therefore also by divine decree) they cannot be causally effective. Even if we reject, or at least ignore, the limits I have set to the causal efficacy of prayer, we can still see other reasons why a request may not be granted. The request may be morally wrong either *per se* or in its motivation. Even spiritual requests can be wrongly motivated. A request may be based on a purely humanistic view of what is good for us or for other people. There is also the fact that many requests are mutually incompatible so that they cannot be answered simultaneously. Thus where and when one person prays for sun, another person may pray for rain. Finally, God may refuse to grant a request for a reason or reasons known only to him.

In drawing this discussion of petitionary and intercessory prayer to a close I shall examine the often used phrase 'the power of prayer'. Obviously our petitions and intercessions have power in so far as they have causal efficacy. Yet the concept of prayer's power has these dangers. (i) It can suggest that through prayer we are able to change God's will whereas in fact any causal connection between our requests and their fulfilment is due solely to his will. (ii) The concept can lead us into the error of thinking that the likelihood of a request being granted is in proportion to the emotional intensity with which it is made or to the number of people who make it. (iii) The concept can produce the error of thinking that prayer in itself, quite apart from divine action in response to it, influences other people by some kind of psychic energy. (iv) Even when these errors are avoided, the concept can lead us to seek a verification of God's activity in the occurrence of events for which we have prayed. Unanswered prayers then expose the believer to the falsification of claims he makes for prayer's power. Ultimately we must think of the power belonging to prayer of all kinds in terms not of man but of God, and in terms not of external effects but of his presence in the soul. Our prayers are true and effective to the extent that they are empowered by the Holy Spirit. And the goal of our prayers both for ourselves and for other people should be that the Holy Spirit may transform us in the likeness of Christ.

Finally we must see the petitionary and intercessory modes of prayer in relation to, first, the other modes of vocal prayer, and, secondly, mental prayer. With regard to the first it is worth noting that all modes of vocal prayer are (or can be) causally effective in the sense that they cause (or can cause) us to experience God and to dispose ourselves for the reception of his grace. Secondly, all modes of vocal prayer, and especially petitions, need to be complemented by mental prayer in the simple form (obtainable by all Christians) of recollecting that we are in the presence of God. William Barclay put it thus in an autobiography he wrote shortly before his death.

> Real prayer is simply being in the presence of God. When I am in trouble, and when I go to my friend, I don't want anything from him except himself. I just want to be with him for a time, to feel his comradeship, his concern, his caring round me and about me, and then to go out to a world warmer because I spent an hour with him. It must be that way with me and God.[21]

Barclay's affirmation does not imply any disparagement of petitionary prayer; for the primary aim of the latter is to ask for spiritual gifts; and God, in the person of the Holy Spirit, imparts himself along with these gifts.

This, then, concludes my survey of vocal prayer in its five main forms of adoration, thanksgiving, confession, petition, and intercession. However, there are three further forms that must be mentioned. These are prayers of dedication, submission, and commitment which are closely related to each other.

In prayers of dedication one can dedicate either oneself or another person (such as an infant who cannot dedicate himself) or a thing (such as a church building). I am now concerned with the first—the dedication of oneself (or ourselves if a group of Christians is involved) to God. Prayers of dedication can occur at various points in the Christian life. There are three points in the liturgy where such prayers are especially appropriate: after confession, after the offertory, and after the act of communion in the eucharist. The idea of dedication is closely connected with the ideas of service and sacrifice. We dedicate ourselves to God's service and offer our lives as a sacrifice to him. These two ideas are brought together in Romans 12:1 (that can be easily converted into a prayer): 'I beseech you, therefore, brethren by the mercies of God that you present your bodies a living sacrifice, holy, acceptable to God, which is your reasonable service'. (AV)

Next there are prayers of submission. These take two forms. The first is covered by the idea of dedication. We must submit ourselves to God in the sense of dedicating ourselves to his service and offering our lives as a sacrifice to him. Secondly, we must submit ourselves to God's will in all those adverse circumstances which we cannot change but must simply endure. Furthermore, submission is required in all our petitions for the occurrence of events; for we must qualify these petitions with the words 'if it is in accordance with thy will'. And we must be ready to accept God's will if our petitions are not granted.

Lastly, there are prayers of commitment. The commitment of ourselves to God is involved in prayers of dedication and submission. We commit ourselves to God whenever we dedicate ourselves to him or submit to his will. Yet I now have in mind the commitment of ourselves to God's providential care in all the circumstances of our lives. Acts of such commitment ought to occur regularly in private prayer. But they are especially required *in extremis*. Here again we are called on to follow the example of Christ. Just as we must imitate his submission to God's will in Gethsemane, so we must imitate his commitment of himself to God's care at Calvary when, despite his cry of dereliction, he prayed immediately before his death: 'Father, into thy hands I commit my spirit'.[22]

CHAPTER FOUR

THE LORD'S PRAYER

Any book covering the basis of Christian prayer would be incomplete without a discussion of the Lord's Prayer. Throughout the history of the Church a pre-eminent place has been assigned to this prayer in terms of both its origin and its content. Its origin as a prayer given by Jesus to his disciples clearly endows it with an authority that cannot be possessed by any other prayer. So far as content goes there is Aquinas's statement that 'the Lord's Prayer is the best of all because, as Augustine says, "If we pray rightly and fittingly we can say nothing else but what is contained in the Lord's Prayer"'.[1] The reverence in which the early Christians held the prayer is shown by the fact (to which Jeremias[2] draws our attention) that for them the recitation of the prayer was a privilege reserved for baptised members of the Church, so that the prayer was called 'the prayer of believers' (in contrast with the modern view that the prayer is meant for everyone). As a later example of Christian reverence for the prayer Jeremias cites the words of the Roman mass (to which there are parallels in non-Roman forms of the eucharistic liturgy): 'We make bold to say (*audemus dicere*) "Our Father"'.

79

However, we are at once confronted with a critical problem. There are two versions of the prayer, the one according to Matthew and the other according to Luke. These differ both in setting and in content. In Matthew's Gospel the prayer occurs after general instruction on prayer that Jesus gives in the Sermon on the Mount. In Luke's Gospel Jesus gives the prayer in answer to the request of his disciples, 'Lord, teach us to pray, as John taught his disciples'. So far as content goes, apart from minor differences of wording, the main difference is that Matthew includes clauses that are not found in Luke. Here are the two versions of the prayer with Matthew's additions underlined.

MATTHEW 6: 9–13	LUKE 11: 2–4
<u>Our</u> Father <u>who art in heaven,</u>	Father,
Hallowed be thy name.	Hallowed be thy name.
Thy kingdom come,	Thy kingdom come.
<u>Thy will be done</u>	
<u>On earth as it is in heaven.</u>	
Give us <u>this day</u> our	Give us each day our
daily bread.	daily bread.
And forgive us our <u>debts</u>	And forgive us our sins,
<u>As</u> we also <u>have forgiven our debtors.</u>	for we also forgive everyone who is indebted to us.
And lead us not into temptation	And lead us not into temptation.
<u>But deliver us from evil.</u>	

In the company of very many (perhaps most) New Testament scholars, I hold that, although at some points the Matthean version of the prayer may be preferable to the Lucan one, the latter is preferable on the two major points I mentioned. First, there is the setting. Matthew's setting reflects the evangelist's tendency to bring together various sayings of Jesus within one sermon and thereby to represent him as the teacher of a new law; but Luke's placing of the prayer as an answer to the disciples' question fits in with the fact (noted by Jeremias) that other religious groups of the day, such as the Pharisees and Essenes, had their distinctive prayers. Secondly, and more importantly, there is the content. Where Matthew's version of the prayer contains clauses not found in Luke's version it is reasonable to regard Luke's version as being historically more reliable on these grounds. It is intrinsically more likely that the clauses were added than that they were omitted; their addition is intelligible as an attempt either to elucidate a clause or to harmonise it with Jewish usage; and the Matthean version, which on account of its balance and rhythm is easier to recite corporately, bears the marks of liturgical expansion.

However, even if this assessment of the two Gospels is correct, it does not follow that the Matthean additions can be ignored. On the contrary an exposition of the prayer must include these additions for the following reasons. First, although we must attempt to discover as far as possible the words that Jesus spoke, we must also pay attention to the ways in which these words were developed and understood by the apostolic church. Secondly, the longer, the Matthean version of the prayer, is the one that has been traditionally used both in public worship and in private devotion.

Thirdly, the clauses found in Matthew but not in Luke contribute towards our understanding of the prayer.

This brings me to an exegetical (or perhaps I should say hermeneutical) principle that affects Jesus' teaching as a whole. Although in expounding the Lord's Prayer we must attempt to discover the meaning it had for Jesus himself when he uttered it, we must also interpret it in the light of his whole ensuing ministry that includes his death, his resurrection, his exaltation, and his gift of the Holy Spirit. We must therefore take account of the interpretation of his person, words, and deeds that was given by the apostolic church. I have already illustrated this principle with regard to Jesus' teaching on prayer when I said that we must interpret the synoptic promise 'Ask and you shall receive' in the light of the Johannine qualification that the Father will grant whatever we ask in his name or the name of Christ his Son.

I shall therefore expound the prayer in both its versions and in the light of the New Testament's total witness to Christ.

The beginning of the Lord's Prayer contains the first of the main differences between the two versions. Whereas Luke has simply 'Father (*pater*)', Matthew adds 'our' before 'Father' and 'who art in heaven' after it. The Lucan version is here preferable for the reason that to address God simply as 'father' was not customary among the Jews because this, being the way in which children addressed their human fathers, was considered to be too intimate a way of addressing the holy God. Jeremias claimed that he had not found a parallel in the whole literature of Judaism. That the mode of address was novel (or at least highly unusual) is indicated by the fact that Paul retained the Aramaic *Abba* as a way of addressing God although he wrote in Greek to Greek-speaking converts.[3] To the Lucan opening of the prayer we must add the fact that the Evangelists record that Jesus himself addressed God simply as 'Father'. He was therefore authorising his disciples to address God in the same intimate way in which he addressed him. He was also thereby inviting them to share in his own relation to God as his Father.

In order to understand fully the invocation of God as, simply, 'Father,' we must place it in the context of the statements that the New Testament elsewhere makes concerning Christ as, first, the incarnate Son of God, and, secondly, one who imparts the Holy Spirit to believers.

First then, there is the Incarnation. This forms the basis of Christ's usage in addressing God simply as Father. The Incarnation thereby also forms the basis of the use of 'Father' by his disciples. Once we grant the uniqueness of Jesus as the incarnation of the divine Son, the uniqueness of the invocation of God as 'Father' both by him and, derivatively, by his disciples is assured. It would remain even if it could be demonstrated that Jews were in the habit of calling God 'Father' in prayer. The decisive evidence here is provided by the Johannine writings. In the prologue to the fourth Gospel the author affirms that Jesus was the incarnation of the eternal Son and Word of the Father. As such Jesus confers a new status on his disciples: 'To all who received him, who believed in his name he gave power to become children of God; who were born, not of blood nor of the will of the flesh nor of the will of man, but of God'.[4] The teaching of I John is summed up in the first verse of an often sung paraphrase: 'Behold the amazing gift of love the Father has bestowed on us, the sinful sons of men, to call us sons of God'.

Next the disciples' invocation of God as Father is confirmed by the action of the Holy Spirit who testifies to their status as sons of God 'by adoption and grace' in imitation of the divine Sonship that Christ possesses by nature. This is affirmed in two Pauline passages to which I have referred. In Galatians 4:6 Paul wrote, 'Because you are sons, God has sent the Spirit of his Son into our hearts, crying "Abba, Father"'. Later he wrote this in

Romans 8:15–17: 'When we cry "Abba, Father" it is the Spirit himself bearing witness with our spirit that we are children of God, and if children, then heirs, heirs of God and fellow heirs with Christ, provided we suffer with him, in order that we may also be glorified with him'.

The invocation of God as 'Father' thus has the trinitarian character that distinguishes Christian prayer as a whole. We address God as Father in the Son and through the Holy Spirit. This explains two factors about the Lord's Prayer that I noted in my introduction to this chapter. In the ancient Church the prayer was not meant for everyone; it was a prayer for disciples; it was meant for those who had accepted God's revelation in Christ. Again, the trinitarian pattern explains why Christians speak of being 'bold' to say 'Our Father'. We have no innate right to address God with the intimacy with which the incarnate Son addressed him. Our right to do so is constituted, first, by the words of Jesus in giving his disciples this prayer, and, secondly, by the inner testimony of the Holy Spirit whom he sends.

Furthermore, we have here an illustration of the hermeneutical principle that I have already noted. We must interpret the Lord's prayer in the light of not only the meaning that it had for Jesus when he uttered it but also the meaning that it has when it is seen in the light of apostolic teaching. This points to another principle. Jesus' earthly ministry was incomplete until the saving events that followed it. Therefore everything he said and did had a proleptic character. It looked forward, for its final meaning and validation, to his death, resurrection, and sending of the Holy Spirit. The role of the Holy Spirit is crucial here (as it is elsewhere). He confirms the gift of sonship implied in the Lord's Prayer's use of Abba. He does so by uniting believers with Christ and through

Christ with the Father in a way that was not possible before Christ's death and resurrection.

Can we, then, validly speak of God as the Father of all men (not only of Christ and his disciples)? Whether Jesus spoke thus has been a matter of dispute among scholars. But in the New Testament epistles God's fatherhood is certainly spoken of in universal terms. The author of the Epistle to the Ephesians writes of 'one God and Father of us all'.[5] The author of the Epistle to the Hebrews describes God as 'the Father of spirits',[6] and James call him 'the Father of lights'.[7] There is therefore biblical warrant for non-Christians speaking (as many in the ancient world, such as Plato and the Stoics, did in fact speak) of God as Father. The symbol is a wholly appropriate way of designating God's creativity, sovereignty and care. The principle of analogy clearly holds here. Just as a human father produces, controls, and cares for, his children, so *eminentiori modo* God creates, controls, and cares for his human creatures.

Nevertheless, Jesus offers us a new, supernatural, relation to God as Father by our union with him. It is this relation that imparts both a final meaning and a final uniqueness to the Christian invocation of God as Father. The distinctiveness of Christian usage here emerges from a consideration of the linkage between God's fatherhood and his creativity. Paul established the linkage when he wrote of 'one God, the Father, from whom are all things'.[8] Later both the Nicene and the Apostles' creeds profess belief in 'the Father Almighty' as the creator of all things. Every theist can accept these statements. But they acquire a new and distinctively Christian meaning when they are interpreted through the doctrines of the Trinity and the Incarnation according to which God is primarily and essentially the Father of the Son through whom he made all things and who became man in Christ.

85

Paul adumbrated this interpretation when he added the words 'and one Lord, Jesus Christ, through whom are all things'.

The distinctive meaning of the opening of the Lord's Prayer in Luke's version (that is, simply 'Father') is blunted by the Matthean additions of 'our' before 'Father' and 'who art in heaven' after it—additions that bring Jesus' teaching into conformity with Jewish usage. Yet the Matthean version is the one that has been constantly recited. Therefore, if only for this reason, it merits consideration. Moreover, the words 'who art in heaven' have value in reminding us that the God whom we address as Father far transcends us in his infinite goodness, wisdom and power. Jesus himself affirmed this transcendence at one point in his ministry when, after addressing God as 'Father', he added the words 'Lord of heaven and earth'.[9] The transcendent quality of God's fatherhood was further brought out when 'Father' came to signify the first person of the Godhead and the one who creates all things *ex nihilo*.

The transcendence of God is affirmed by the following words which are the same in both versions of the prayer, and which complement the invocation of God as, simply, 'Father'. The words are 'hallowed be thy name'.

The verb here translated 'hallowed' is connected with the Greek adjective *hagios* meaning holy or sacred. And holiness is first and foremost a property of God. To hallow is to treat as holy. The petition can therefore be translated as 'thy name be treated as holy'. Since the appropriate attitude to the holy God is one of reverence, the petition can also be translated as 'thy name be held in reverence' or, more simply, 'thy name be revered'.

Next, there is the noun 'name'. We are apt to think of a name as being wholly distinct from, or other than, the object named, and to suppose that the object would be the same if it had another name. Thus I tend to think that my friend John would be the same if he had been called Michael or David. The ancient Jews thought otherwise. For them a person's name expressed the nature of the person named. Especially God's name expressed his nature. Therefore in the Bible God's 'name' is often equivalent to God himself.

The whole petition has been summed up thus.

> To hallow is to treat as holy, to honour, to revere. In the Bible "the name" means "the nature". God's name is his nature as made known to man. God has made himself known to men—has spelt out his great name to them—in nature, in conscience, in his prophets, in his mighty acts in history, above all in Jesus Christ his only Son. So, in this petition we pray that men may reverence God in all these ways in which he reveals himself.[10]

What does it mean for us to revere God's name? Most obviously it means that we must refrain from using his name or the name of Christ casually as a swear word or expletive. This usage occurs frequently today. It is not always a grave matter—thus a person who says 'good God' to express surprise or indignation need not intend the expression seriously; and he or she may be horrified by the idea of committing blasphemy. Nevertheless, such expressions ought to be avoided by Christians for whom 'God' signifies the holy creator and 'Christ' signifies his incarnate Son.

However, there are more profound ways in which Christians are required to reverence God's name. Here are three of them. First, when we remember that reverence is akin to worship, and that in Hebraic usage the name of God is virtually equivalent to God himself, we can see that this petition points to prayer in the form of adoration. The Lord's prayer does not include either adoration or thanksgiving. Yet as a Jew Jesus would have taken these forms of prayer for granted. And the first is implied by this petition.

The second point at which the words 'hallowed be thy name' bear on the nature of prayer concerns the ways in which we formulate our petitions. Here I need only repeat what I said in the preceding chapter. In asking God for something, especially for the occurrence of an event or state of affairs, we must avoid any tendency to think that we can 'use' God for obtaining what we consider to be conducive to our temporal well-being. To reverence God's name here means that we ask him to grant us this or that only if to grant it is in accordance with his will.

The third way in which we are required to reverence God's name is of particular relevance to preachers and theologians. We must constantly remember that God, in both his being and his acts, ultimately surpasses our understanding. Therefore a 'reverent agnosticism' ought to characterise our attempts to speak of him and his providence. This is especially so when we are considering the problem of evil. Of course we must tackle the problem as far as we can with the help of both reason and revelation. Yet our reverence for God is bound to exclude any hope of putting ourselves in the position of God deciding to create a world with or without evil (or a world with or without evil of this or that kind). In fact, quite apart from the theological problem constituted by evil, a spirit of 'reverent agnosticism' pervades prayer in the form of adoration.

An examination of the words 'hallowed be thy name' in terms of their background reveals a further reference that is rarely in the minds of those who recite the Lord's Prayer today. The Jews thought of God himself hallowing, or sanctifying, his name. By this they meant that God would so act that all men would recognise him for what he is, the holy creator and judge of all mankind. Ezekiel expressed it thus:

> And I will vindicate the holiness of my great name, which has been profaned among the nations and which you have profaned among them; and the nations will know that I am the Lord, says the Lord God, when through you I vindicate my holiness before their eyes.[11]

This provides a point of transition to the next petition which is 'thy kingdom come'.

The words 'thy kingdom come' occur in both versions of the prayer. Despite the large amount that has been written on Jewish and early Christian concepts of God's kingdom, and despite differences of scholarly opinion, the main points relevant to an understanding of this petition are clear.

It is necessary to begin with two distinctions. The first is between two meanings of the word *basileia* in the Greek of the New Testament. This can be translated either 'reign' or 'kingdom'. Both translations are required in various contexts; but 'reign' is the dominant meaning of the word. The two meanings are complementary. Thus in secular usage a king's reign implies a kingdom or sphere over which his reign is exercised, and the idea of a kingdom implies the idea of a monarch who rules over it.

The second distinction is between two forms of God's rule. As the creator, God is sovereign over the whole world. But this universal sovereignty of God is not the meaning of kingdom in the New Testament (especially the Gospels). This meaning has its origin in the eschatological expectations of Judaism. At the time of Jesus, and for many years previously, the Jews hoped that one day God would establish his reign fully over Israel and, through Israel, over mankind as a whole. In that day evil would be abolished; Israel, that had so often been disobedient, would wholly obey God's law; and there would be one perfect society characterised by righteousness, peace and joy. The Jews conceived this coming kingdom variously. A good summary is given as follows by C. F. Evans in his commentary on the Lord's Prayer.

> There was more than one view of what was involved. Some saw it in political terms; God would bring it about that the nation was freed from foreign yoke to become a people devoted to him under his vicegerent, a new David. Others, a great many of the Pharisees for example, saw it more as a spiritual renewal, by which God would bring about a complete devotion to his will as it was expressed in the divine law of Moses and in all that the law implied. Others, who despaired of the world as hopelessly evil, saw it as God's miraculous transformation of the present order of things and as a new heaven and a new earth. In one way or another Jewish faith came to be orientated towards this hope, and at times to tremble on the brink of its realisation. The Jewish rabbis just before or contemporary with Jesus were the first to use the actual phrase 'the kingdom of God', or, more usually, in order to avoid from reverence the mention of God, 'the kingdom of heaven', as generally in Matthew's Gospel.[12]

When we turn to the Synoptic Gospels we find that Jesus proclaimed both that this expected kingdom had come in his ministry and that it was still to come. In the technical language used by New Testament scholars, Jesus taught both a 'realised' and a 'futurist' eschatology.

Perhaps the clearest example of realised eschatology is when Jesus appeals to his exorcisms as signs that God's kingdom has come. 'If it is by the Spirit of God that I cast out demons, then the kingdom of God has come upon you'.[13] We must not confine the synoptic evidence for realised eschatology to texts that explicitly mention the kingdom. We must also reckon with other texts in which Jesus affirms or implies that the new age of Jewish prophecy has dawned in him. But Jesus also refers to the kingdom as something in the future. This petition in the Lord's Prayer is an example. Another example is Mark 9:1 where Jesus says that 'there are some standing here who shall not taste death before they see the kingdom of God come with power'. At other places where the kingdom is mentioned, it is not always clear whether a present or a future reference is intended.

These two forms of eschatology occur also in the Epistles. The latter, by comparison with the Gospels, contain few references to the kingdom. This is largely because for the first Christians the reign of God, the new age that Christ proclaimed, was embodied in Christ himself. Yet the same combination of the present and the future that marked the teaching of Jesus also marked the outlook of the apostolic church. Just as Jesus taught that the kingdom was both present and yet to come, so his disciples believed both that he inaugurated the new age by his saving acts and that the new age awaited its final consummation in a final act whereby he would come again in glory and bring history to its end. This can be re-expressed by saying that for the first Christians God's reign in Christ had the marks of both 'the already' and 'the not yet'. It had already been established perfectly in Christ's own person; it is established too in the lives of Christians in so far as they have the Spirit of Christ; but it will not be fully present until God's last apocalypse in

Christ at the end of history. Meanwhile 'the age to come' co-exists with 'this age' and all the evil that the latter contains.

To return to the Lord's Prayer, it is the futurist form of eschatology that Jesus here had in mind. He tells his disciples to pray for the kingdom that is yet to come. More precisely, there is widespread agreement among exegetes that Jesus meant the kingdom's final advent, its consummation through a divine act whereby 'this age' will pass away and all mankind will be subject to God's sovereignty within the new age of which the prophets spoke. C.F. Evans notes that the tense of the Greek verb (the aorist imperative *elthatō*) suggests what will come once and for all. Earlier T.W. Manson gave this interpretation in his *The Sayings of Jesus*.

> The coming of the kingdom here is certainly the final consummation. In the fullest sense the kingdom is still future and an object of hope rather than experience. The petition is that the hope may be fulfilled. In the primitive church this hope is bound up with the expectation of the return of the risen Lord: and the early Christian equivalent to 'thy kingdom come' is *maranatha*—come our Lord.[14]

Moreover some texts in the Gospels (such as Mark 9:1) suggest that Jesus expected this final consummation soon, within the lifetime of some among his listeners. Undoubtedly this expectation, together with the hope of Christ's imminent return in glory, was cherished by Christians in the early days of the Church.

This petition differs from other petitions in the prayer in two closely related respects. First, it depends more than they do on an understanding of the Jewish background. Secondly, it raises the question of the extent to which we can make Jewish and early Christian eschatology our own. What, then, does the petition mean for us today? We no longer expect an imminent end of history and the final advent of the kingdom. In fact, the expectation faded in the ancient Church that was forced to come to terms with the continuance of secular society. Again, many Christians today would take the associated belief in Christ's last coming symbolically, not with the literalism with which it has often been taken. Nevertheless, the petition enshrines an essential, and so an abiding, element in Christian hope. All Christians must hope for a final establishment of the new age that Christ instituted by his life, death, resurrection, and gift of the Holy Spirit. All can hope for this even when they differ in other respects in their views on 'last things'. All too can hope for it even if they are agnostic concerning the time and manner of its coming.

This petition, then, is a prayer for the future and final advent of the kingdom that Christ inaugurated. Certainly the 'realised' strain in New Testament eschatology compels Christians to pray also for the coming of the kingdom here and now, within the confines of history. In so far as Christians remain sinners who have never submitted themselves wholly to God's reign in Christ they must pray primarily for its coming in themselves both individually and corporately (as members of the Church that, though not identical with the kingdom, is a divinely appointed sign of it). Next Christians must pray that those who do not now acknowledge God's reign in Christ may come to do so. In these ways Christians can validly pray for the 'extension' of God's kingdom on earth. Nevertheless, the eschatology of the New Testament, confirmed by nearly twenty centuries of Christianity, requires the belief that God's reign will not come fully within history. 'This age' and 'the age to come', good and evil (even among Christians), Christians and non-Christians, will co-exist

93

until the end. For the kingdom's full advent we await a new and final act of God for which Jesus bids us pray in this petition.

Next there are the words 'thy will be done, on earth as it is in heaven'. Although these words do not occur in Luke and can be reasonably regarded as a Matthean addition, they require comment for these reasons. They are part of the prayer that is normally recited; the concept of God's will is an essential element in both the Jewish and the Christian forms of theism; and the desire for the advent of God's reign, that is expressed in the previous petitions is inseparable from the desire that his will be done among those over whom he reigns. The petition has two meanings. The first is that we may do God's will in our own choices and actions (especially those of a distinctively moral kind). The second meaning is that God's will be done in and through those events over which we have no control. Therefore, as I have more than once stated and stressed, whenever we pray for something to occur (or not to occur) we must always add the qualification 'if it is in accordance with thy will'.

The first meaning of this petition includes (or at least entails) the further petition that God may give us both the illumination and the strength to obey his will. It is a Christian axiom that God will grant us both the illumination and the strength if we ask him. Yet the idea of divine illumination calls for comment. The main principles here, I maintain, are these. In the combined light of reason, scripture, and tradition, most Christians for most of the time need have no doubt where their duty lies and so what is God's will for them. Yet even here they must pray for his illumination because they can easily be blinded to their duty by the original sin that still remains in them. Moreover there are cases in which we can have reasonable cause for moral doubt. Two examples are when

94

there is a conflict between moral claims and when there is moral disagreement between Christians. Again, we are sometimes confronted with choices affecting the whole course of our lives when we are uncertain how we ought to choose. Then there is a special need to pray for the illumination of the Holy Spirit. Yet God does not illumine us by suppressing our faculties of reason and conscience that he himself has given us as means of perceiving what is true and right. Rather he sharpens these faculties and gives them powers of perception that they would not otherwise possess. He does not, therefore, illumine us in some supra-rational manner that bears beyond all doubt the marks of his illumination and that thus exempts from any possibility of error. These facts have the following consequences. First, even if we find a clarification of judgement after praying about a perplexing matter, our judgement is still subject to rational testing. Let us take the case of a person who claims that, despite previous doubt, he feels guided through prayer to offer himself for ordination. His vocation still needs to be tested by the Church. Secondly, we cannot validly take anything to be God's will and so an answer to a prayer for his illumination if it is contrary to our sense of what is morally required; for it is always God's will that conscience should be obeyed. Thus it would be both religiously and morally wrong for a pacifist to claim that he has been 'guided' to become a non-pacifist although he is still convinced by the arguments for pacifism.

According to the second meaning of the petition we pray that God's will be done in those events over which we have no control. This meaning is especially relevant to situations that cause us (or other people) suffering and where our prayers for the removal of the suffering are unanswered. To pray in such situations that God's will be done entails the further prayer that we may have grace to resign ourselves to God's will in the knowledge that he is in control of all things and that there is no evil from which he cannot bring good, if not in this world, then in the next. Christians pray for this after the example of Christ. He was prepared to accept the cross if it was God's will for him. Also his sufferings constituted the supreme case of God bringing good out of evil both because they were the price of our redemption and because they were succeeded by the glory of the resurrection.

However, Christians have sometimes advocated a premature resignation. God does not rejoice in suffering or will it for its own sake. Therefore, he does not wish us to be resigned to it as if it were in all cases irremovable by his decree. On the contrary it is his will that we should attempt to remove or at least mitigate it as far as possible. So far as the sufferings of other people are concerned this attempt is a self-evident demand of Christian compassion. God requires us to resign ourselves to suffering and to his will for us in it only to the extent that it is not amenable to removal or mitigation. Therefore, Christians must pray for the capacity to distinguish between those ills that are and those that are not thus amenable. This was expressed by Reinhold Niebuhr as follows in a prayer that is applicable to various situations. 'God, give us grace to accept with serenity the things that cannot be changed, courage to change the things that should be changed, and the wisdom to distinguish the one from the other'.[15]

'Thy will be done', when we refer it to ourselves, is the most costly of petitions for anyone who utters it sincerely and with a full recognition of all it entails. To do God's will means to perform his commandments with inner purity of motive and intention as well as with outer rectitude; it means to love God perfectly and one's neighbour as oneself; it means enduring pain, frustration, injustice, and so on with faith in God's overruling providence. In all these ways it means practising the self-renunciation that Jesus enjoined thus: 'If any man would come after me, let him deny himself and take up his cross and follow me'.[16] Yet self-will and self-seeking so often prevent us from doing or even desiring to do God's will. And so this petition leads to a prayer for forgiveness which is the theme of a later petition in the Lord's prayer.

The next petition is 'Give us this day our daily bread'. I have quoted and I shall consider the petition in its familiar Matthean version. I shall retain the traditional 'daily' as the translation of the Greek *epiousion*. Also I shall follow the normal practice of taking 'bread' in its straightforward, materialistic, sense to signify the ordinary, material, bread that we habitually eat. Some commentators (including both ancient and modern ones) have given the word a 'spiritual' interpretation. Thus it has been held to signify Christ who, according to the fourth Gospel, called himself 'the bread of life'. But the natural and simple sense of the word, and one that is free from any preconceived ideas, is the materialistic one that is usually accepted without question. Admittedly all the other petitions in the Lord's Prayer are for spiritual blessings; but we have no right to give this petition a spiritual sense simply in order to produce uniformity. Admittedly too, Christ is elsewhere recorded as affirming that 'man shall not live by bread alone, but by every word that proceeds from the mouth of God';[17] and that we must 'not labour for the food which perishes, but for the food which endures to eternal life'.[18] Again Jesus tells us not to be anxious for material things but to seek first God's kingdom and his righteousness.[19] And I have often emphasised the primacy of spiritual petitions in Christian prayer. Nevertheless, we have material as well as spiritual needs. The former needs are those that Jesus envisages here in accordance both with the Hebraic stress on man's psycho-somatic unity and with his own practice of healing sickness of body as well as sickness of soul.

On these assumptions this petition raises two questions. The first is one with which I have already dealt, and so I shall now merely restate my answer. Our daily bread depends on elements in physical nature that operate independently of our prayers and that offer scope for the formulation of scientifically established laws. It depends on seed-time and harvest which in turn depend on the state of the soil and the weather. Jesus himself affirmed the operation of God's universal and undiscriminating providence when he said that God 'makes his sun rise on the evil and on the good, and sends rain on the just and on the unjust'.[19] How, then, can prayer make a difference to (or causally affect) the natural processes on which our daily bread depends? Surely here prayer cannot be causally effective. Nevertheless, Christians have found it wholly natural to offer this petition. The reason is that the petition is an inevitable way of expressing our dependence on God for the continuance of those processes that enable bread to be produced. To put it negatively, the petition for our daily bread is an inevitable way of averting the spiritual danger of taking God's material gifts for granted.

The second question raised by this petition is an acute and, in my opinion, more difficult one. In answering the first question I have taken for granted the normal state of Europeans who can assume that the processes of nature and the distribution of wealth will give them enough to eat. Some harvests are better than others, and there is still an unacceptable gap between the very rich and the very poor. Nevertheless, there is no need for anyone to starve for lack of bread or some basic equivalent, except perhaps temporarily and in unusual circumstances.

Yet in other parts of the world large numbers of men, women and children are dying of starvation either because of famine (which may be exacerbated by war) or because of extreme poverty. Let us take as an example an African peasant in an area struck by famine. How can he pray for his daily bread? Can he pray for a miracle? On this I must refer to what I said earlier concerning prayer and miracles. One solution of the problem could be that in such a situation a person is asking God, not to perform a miracle, but to move the hearts of people elsewhere so that they will send food (together with other, especially medical, aid) to relieve suffering and stave off death. This, however, introduces a change into the petition; it involves further questions raised by prayers for God to influence other people; and the help requested may not come or not come in time.

Here, therefore, we have the possibility of unanswered prayer. Having discussed the question of unanswered prayer I now wish only to offer the following observation. The case I have been considering is not unique. There are countless prayers, fervently offered by devout Christians in similar circumstances, that are unanswered. Thus a Western Christian who enjoys every material benefit may pray for the recovery of his or her sick child; but the child may die; and to a parent it makes no difference in the end whether his or her child dies of famine or of cancer. Of course the scale and squalor of suffering in an African famine exceed anything we know in the West; but so far as unanswered prayer goes the principle is the same.

My final comments are of general application but are specially relevant to the petition I have been considering. First, in praying for our daily bread (as in offering other petitions) we must bear in mind that in all things we are required to co-operate with God through an exercise of the powers with which he has endowed us. The best of harvests is useless until human effort and skill have converted it into bread. Secondly, our prayers for ourselves are inseparable from our prayers for others; and our prayers for others include prayers that we may help them according to their needs. These two facts mean that this petition leads to a prayer for grace to do all that is in our power to feed the hungry, whoever and wherever they may be.

The next petition is a prayer for forgiveness. The two versions here differ slightly. Matthew's is 'forgive us our debts, as we also have forgiven our debtors'. Luke's is 'forgive us our sins, for we also forgive everyone who is indebted to us'. Two points of exegesis must be noted. First, both versions use the language of debt. 'Debt' here is a financial metaphor that Jesus took from Judaism and that he used on other occasions. The idea is that men and women as God's creatures, and especially Israel as the people of his covenant, are under an obligation to obey his law. But through their sin they have failed to meet the obligation; they have fallen into arrears of duty; this is the debt. God then remits or cancels the debt (or 'writes it off'). This remission is his forgiveness.

Secondly, both Matthew and Luke link God's forgiveness of us with our forgiveness of each other. According to Matthew, Jesus taught that our forgiveness of each other is a condition of God's forgiveness of us. 'If you do not forgive men their trespasses, neither will your Father forgive your trespasses'.[20] Jesus states the same condition in his parable of the unmerciful servant. God's forgiveness is unconditional in so far as, first, he is always ready to offer it, and, secondly, it is a wholly unmerited gift. Yet our capacity to receive his forgiveness is conditional upon our forgiveness of each other. Another condition (not mentioned in the prayer but presupposed by it) is that we repent. The two conditions are related in that an unforgiving spirit is itself a sin for which our repentance is required. Unless these two conditions are met God's forgiveness of sins becomes a condonation of them. It would mean that he treated sin lightly, as being of no great account. The moral order would then be violated. It would be outrageous if God forgave sins while the sinner remained unforgiving and impenitent. It would also do spiritual and moral harm to those forgiven by blinding them to the seriousness of their sins and even encouraging them to remain in them.

I think it likely that many of us recite this petition without being fully aware of its reference to our forgiveness of each other. One reason for this could be that we subconsciously evade the challenge it presents. Another reason could be that although Christian teaching on forgiveness relates it constantly to the necessity for repentance it does not nearly so often relate it to the necessity for forgiving each other. In fact, however, although the condition 'unforgiving, unforgiven' must remain, if people, with a due sense of their own sins and hatred of them, realise the wonder of God's forgiveness, they will inevitably forgive their fellow human beings.

What, then, does God's forgiveness mean? In what does it consist? Its main ingredients are these (that are also present, *mutatis mutandis*, in our forgiveness of each other). First, God treats the sinner as if the sin had not occurred; he wipes out the debt; and he thereby removes the burden of guilt that the consciousness of sin engenders. All this is covered by the ideas of remission, pardon, and absolution. Secondly, and as a consequence, God does not 'remember' our sins in the sense of continuing to hold them against us. Thirdly, by forgiving us he renews the personal relationship with us that our sin has broken. Paul expresses this renewal through the concept of justification. For him, to say that God 'justifies' us through Christ is equivalent to saying that through the

101

forgiveness he offers us in Christ, he accepts us as we are and restores us to the relation with him that he intends for us. God does this because, being pure love, he desires, not the condemnation of the sinner, but the reconciliation of the sinner to himself.

The early Christians considered the forgiveness of sins to be so important for their understanding of the gospel that they stated belief in it as a separate item in both the Apostles' and the Nicene Creeds. So far as prayers for forgiveness are concerned, here are two among the many further examples that could be given both from the Bible and from post-biblical sources. The first is Jesus' parable of the Pharisee and the publican in which he commends the publican (in contrast with the self-righteous Pharisee) for praying 'God, be merciful to me a sinner'.[21] Secondly, there is the 'Jesus prayer' that is central to Orthodox spirituality and that in its standard form runs: 'Lord Jesus Christ, Son of God, have mercy on me'.

The Lord's Prayer ends with the words: 'Lead us not into temptation, but deliver us from evil'. I shall pay attention chiefly to the first half of this petition ('lead us not into temptation') for two reasons. First, it occurs in both versions of the prayer, whereas the words 'deliver us from evil' occur only in Matthew's version. Secondly, the first half of the petition has caused more difficulty than any other part of the prayer, not only for scholars, but also for Christians as a whole.

The Greek word here translated 'temptation' is *peirasmon* which can also be translated 'trial' or 'test'. In many English versions of the Bible, and in the prayer as it is generally recited, the word is rendered 'temptation'. But it can equally well be rendered 'trial' or 'test'. If we adopt the second translation we can render the whole petition as 'put us not to the trial' or 'put us not to the test'. The New English Bible translates 'do not bring us to the test'.

Let us take first the customary rendering, 'lead us not into temptation'. The obvious difficulty with this rendering, if it is not qualified in some way, is that it could suggest that God tempts us to do evil unless we ask him not to do so. But this suggestion is absurd. God never tempts us to do evil; he leads us only to do good. The one who tempts us is Satan. These words in the Epistle of James are directly relevant here. 'Let no one say when he is tempted "I am tempted by God"; for God cannot be tempted with evil and he himself tempts no one; but each person is tempted when he is lured and enticed by his own desire'.[22]

If, then, we render *peirasmon* as 'temptation' we must take it in one of these ways. First, 'do not allow us to be tempted' or 'do not lead us into situations where we are tempted'. The difficulty with this is that although God does not tempt us, he allows us to be tempted and permits situations in which we are tempted. Indeed, there is no situation in which we cannot be tempted. Even the monastic life or the work of the pastoral ministry carries with it its own spiritual and moral dangers. The second interpretation (often given by commentators such as Luther and Calvin) is 'do not let us fall into temptation (or give in to it)'. This, of course, is a perfectly valid petition. We must always ask God for grace to prevent us from yielding to temptation. It is therefore sufficient to take the petition in this plain and simple sense. To the objection that this gives a gloss on or interpretation of the words rather than an exposition of the words themselves, it can be justly replied that some interpretation or gloss is required in order to give the words an acceptable meaning.

Nevertheless, in order to complete the task of exegesis we must consider the second translation of *peirasmon*. This is 'trial' or 'test'. And so the NEB translates 'do not bring us to the test'. The difficulty with this is that God does test us or allow us to be tested. Testing (and testing through temptation), is part of his will for us. This is stated in these two New Testament passages. Earlier in the same chapter from which I have already quoted the author of the Epistle of James wrote this: 'Count it all joy, my brethren, when you meet various trials, for you know that the testing of your faith produces steadfastness'.[23] Again, there is I Peter 1: 6–7 which runs thus: 'In this you rejoice, though now for a little while you may have to suffer various trials, so that the genuineness of your faith, more precious than gold which, though perishable, is tested by fire, may redound to praise, and glory, and honour at the revelation of Jesus Christ.

Therefore once again we are compelled to provide a gloss or further interpretation. Some special test, or some specially severe kind of testing, must be meant. At least one such test can be envisaged. This is where the severity of the test tempts us to some act of betrayal or disloyalty whereby the very basis of our moral or religious life is undermined and our integrity is shattered. As an example of moral betrayal let us consider a member of the French resistance in the Second World War who is tortured by the Gestapo to reveal the name of a colleague. If he reveals it he betrays, not only his colleague, but also the principles that led him to fight Nazism.

The supreme case of religious testing is when our loyalty to God or Christ is threatened by some extreme form of external pressure. The most acute form of such pressure is persecution, to which T. W. Manson (in the company of other exegetes) takes this petition to refer. He notes that for Judaism in the last two centuries B.C., as for Christianity in the first three centuries A.D., persecution was the supreme test because it represented a supreme incentive to apostasy. He then says this: 'What this petition asks therefore is that disciples may not be exposed to trials so severe that their loyalty to God may be undermined.'[24]

Surely knowing our frailty we must ask to be spared such terrible tests as the ones I have mentioned. And there are other severe tests of faith (such as extreme and prolonged pain) that threaten all of us in the course of our ordinary lives. Yet here a difficulty immediately arises (although it is sometimes ignored). Innumerable Christians have been compelled to face extreme trials and tests although they have prayed fervently to be delivered from them. Hence, here again we must envisage the possibility of unanswered prayer. On this it is sufficient to note that Jesus' prayer to be spared his final test of crucifixion was unanswered, and that he asked to be spared it only if this was in accordance with his Father's will.

There remains the second half of the petition (found only in Matthew's Gospel): 'Deliver us from evil'. Here again two translations are possible. The Greek word translated 'evil' can be either masculine or neuter. It can mean either 'the evil one or person (that is, Satan)' or, non-personally, evil as active in the lives of human beings. A good case can be made out for the view that the first meaning is the one that Jesus intended. The verb 'deliver' is suited to a personal object. Also a reference to Satan would fit in well with the religious meaning of 'test' that I gave; for Satan's aim is to seduce us from allegiance to God and Christ. The whole petition could then be paraphrased: 'Do not put us to the final test of our faith; but rescue us from Satan when he tempts us to renounce thee'.

Yet many people today find it hard to believe in the existence of Satan. If we find it so we can take the Greek word in its neuter, impersonal, sense to mean the evil that resides in human minds and wills. Then the second half of the petition presents no problem. We must continually pray to God for deliverance from evil—from the evil that is in ourselves and from the influence of the evil that is in the world around us. We pray for it in the name of Christ who conquered evil on our behalf and who, through the Holy Spirit, enables us to share his victory.

And so we come to the end of the Lord's Prayer. The prayer has often been called 'the pattern prayer'. Obviously it merits this title in so far as it has its origins in the words of Jesus himself. It also merits the title in terms of its content on these three grounds. (i) The prayer is theocentric. We are to pray first for the hallowing of God's name, the coming of his kingdom, and the doing of his will. It is only afterwards that we pray for ourselves (for our daily bread, the forgiveness of our sins, and our deliverance from evil). (ii) With only one exception, the petitions are for spiritual, not material, blessings. (iii) The prayer's invocation of God as 'Father', when this is read in the light of the New Testament as a whole, imparts to the prayer a trinitarian form. We pray to the Father through the Son and by the Holy Spirit. All true Christian prayer has this threefold character.

The Lord's prayer has also been called 'the family prayer'. This description too is appropriate if we mean the Christian family, the Church. The facts that the prayer was originally given by Jesus to his disciples for their distinctive use, that in the early church the prayer was regarded as a privilege conferred by baptism, and that the prayer has been constantly recited at services of the Church—all these facts constitute the prayer as a major means of unifying Christians of various denominations within one community.

CHAPTER FIVE

FURTHER QUESTIONS (I)

I n this chapter and the next I shall discuss various topics that remain. In this chapter I shall discuss the relation between prayer and belief, the relation between prayer and religious experience, the language of prayer, the place of feelings (or emotions) in prayer, difficulties in (or obstacles to) prayer, and a group of questions constituting practical guidance for private prayer. In the next chapter I shall discuss meditation, contemplation, and mystical prayer.

My first topic, then, is the relation between prayer and belief. I stated the basic form of this relation in chapter 1 where I listed those beliefs that are presupposed by Christian prayer. There I divided these beliefs into two categories. First, there are the beliefs that Christians share with other theists. The chief among these are that God is personal, omnipotent, omniscient, immutable, wholly good, and the creator of all things. Next, there are the distinctively Christian beliefs that are embodied in the doctrines of the Trinity, the Incarnation, and the Atonement. God exists in the three persons of Father, Son and Holy Spirit; and in the Son he became man for us men and for our salvation. I shall now develop observations I have made on the trinitarian nature of Christian prayer.

Prayer can be addressed to each of the divine persons; for each possesses fully the nature of the one, indivisible, God. Origen, in his treatise on prayer, held that we should pray to the Father only; but this reflected his subordination of the Spirit to the Son and the Son to the Father (in accordance with the middle Platonists' concept of a hierarchy of being within the divine realm).[1] However, according to the fully developed doctrine of the Trinity that came to be the norm of orthodoxy, the divine persons are coequal. Therefore, prayer can be offered either to each of them separately or to all together. The invocation of all together is especially apt to occur in ascriptions of praise and adoration.

When we address the divine persons individually it is natural for us to follow a long tradition in speaking of (and so to) God the Father as our creator, God the Son as our redeemer, and God the Holy Spirit as our sanctifier. This is a theologically valid way of speaking in so far as these are the distinctive ways in which the divine persons operate and are revealed to us. Yet two counter-balancing facts must be borne in mind. First, all three persons are active in all God's operations. Secondly, although it is appropriate to speak of and to the Father as our creator, he is primarily the Father of the Son through whom he created all things.

Nevertheless, Origen points us to the following truth. The final form of trinitarian prayer is to the Father in the Son and through the Holy Spirit. Although the divine persons are coequal (so that it is proper to pray to each of them or to all together), primacy belongs to the Father. Within the being of God himself (in the 'essential' form of the Trinity) the Father is the source or fount of the godhead (*fons deitatis*). It is by him that the Son is generated; and it is from him that the Spirit proceeds. Within the order of redemption (in the Trinity's 'economic' form) the Father sends the Son, and the Son sends the Spirit. In so far as we are Christians we know the Father in the incarnate Son, Jesus Christ. It is on the authority of the Son, in the prayer he gave to his disciples, that we call God 'Father'. Our right to do so is confirmed by the Holy Spirit who enables us to pray according to the mind of Christ. The revelation of the Father in the Son and through the Holy Spirit leads us back in prayer through the Spirit in the Son to the Father.

The trinitarian nature of Christian prayer affects prayer in all its forms. But it is especially important to note how it affects prayer's petitionary form. The ultimate object of our petitions should be that through the Holy Spirit we become united with the Son in his relation to the Father and so participate in the life of the Trinity. All the virtues for which we pray are granted to us by the Father in the Son through the Holy Spirit. Our petitions for the occurrence, or non-occurrence, of particular events must be governed by our identification, through the Holy Spirit, with the incarnate Son in his readiness to accept his Father's will. Belief in the Trinity also shapes our intercessions for each other as fellow members of the Church. Our final prayer here must be that through the Holy Spirit we may be united to each other by and in the mutual love of the Father and the Son.

I shall next consider the question whether the practice of prayer can determine the content of belief. Can it enable us to choose one belief and reject another? Can it validate or invalidate beliefs? It seems to me that prayer does have these functions. Many reasons can be given in support of Christian beliefs. One reason is that a belief is entailed by experience, worship, and prayer. Therefore beliefs that are affirmed or implied by prayer exert a *prima facie* claim on our assent, although firm assent is justified only if the beliefs are also based on other grounds. Conversely a belief that is incompatible with prayer can be justly rejected if it is also open to criticism on other grounds. I shall illustrate these positive and negative types of relation between prayer and belief by three examples.

First, there is the belief, held by all theists, in God's personality. Prayer validates a personal, as against a non-personal, view of God. In prayer we address God as 'thou' (or 'you'). Our prayers imply belief in God as one who hears our prayers and answers them. A personal view of God is confirmed by Christ who taught his disciples in accordance with his own practice to address God as 'Father'. My second example is taken from Christology. The crucial factor here is prayer in the form of adoration. There are many reasons why the early Church came to affirm belief in Christ's full deity and to embody its belief in the Nicene Creed. But a decisive reason was that Christians felt impelled to accord to Christ the adoration that is due to God alone. M. F. Wiles stated this as follows. 'Whatever the intellectual merits of Dynamic Monarchianism, Origenist subordinationism, and philosophical Arianism, they failed very largely because they did not do justice to Christian apprehension of the Son as a fitting object of worship and adoration'.[2] Thirdly, there is the Augustinian doctrine of predestination. There are many reasons for rejecting this. The relevant reason here is that the doctrine both limits the scope of our intercessions (for it permits us to pray only for the elect) and erodes our confidence in interceding (for only God knows the names of the elect).

This is a point at which it is appropriate to comment in general on the relation between prayer and theology. Although my remarks apply to theology as a whole, I have in mind especially those forms of it that are concerned with the formulation, criticism, and justification of beliefs. Theology and prayer ought to complement each other. On the one hand theology can become a spiritually arid pursuit, a rationative exercise lacking in the sense of divine reality that prayer kindles. On the other hand prayer is no substitute for theology that is an essential requirement of faith as *fides quaerens intellectum* (faith in search of understanding). Again, on the one hand the theologian ought to pray for the Spirit's guidance in his task and to take account of prayer in the formulation of beliefs. On the other hand prayer must be submitted to the kind of doctrinal and philosophical reflection that I am attempting in this book.

The unification of prayer and theology is supremely exemplified by Anselm's *Proslogion*.[3] Anselm begins by invoking God's illumination: 'O Lord my God, teach my heart where and how to seek You'. Later Anselm puts his theological quest in the context of the soul's desire for and love of God: 'Let me seek You in desiring You; let me desire You in seeking You. Let me find You in loving You; let me love You in finding You'. Anselm's ensuing account of God's existence and attributes either takes the form of prayer or is interspersed with prayer. He ends with a prayer containing the following petition. 'O God, I pray, let me know and love You so that I may rejoice in You. And if I cannot in this life fully, let me advance day by day until the point of fullness comes. Let knowledge of You progress in me here, and be made full there. Let love for You grow in me here and be made full there, so that here my joy may be great with expectancy while there being full in realization'. But Anselm does not allow prayer to be a substitute for theological argument. On the contrary he has often been criticised for trusting too far in the powers of purely deductive reasoning in his exposition of Christian beliefs. Rather, for him prayer provides the setting and motivation of theology.

Yet my fundamental presupposition can be queried. Throughout this section (and indeed the book as a whole) I have adhered to the commonly held assumption that prayer presupposes belief in God's existence. Is it, then, reasonable for an unbeliever to pray? Here we must distinguish between atheists and agnostics. It surely would be unreasonable for atheists (by which I mean those who firmly deny God's existence) to pray; and I cannot imagine them doing so. Yet a different case is presented by agnostics (by which I mean those who say that God may exist although they themselves are unable to believe in God's existence). If an agnostic feels driven to pray, it is, I hold, reasonable for him or her to do so. The prayer, 'O God, if you exist help me' need not be either irreverent or absurd. Admittedly, if agnostics prayed only for deliverance from physical danger, and if they forgot about God when the danger had passed, their prayer would be valueless. But if they prayed for spiritual gifts (including the gift of faith), and if they persisted in prayer, their praying is commendable as an acknowledgement of their deepest needs.[4]

The case of an agnostic may seem irrelevant in a book devoted to Christian prayer. Yet a mention of it is necessary because of the extent to which agnosticism is present in the West today. Moreover, it leads to a distinctively Christian problem. Let us consider the case of a Christian who has lost his faith; he has become an agnostic. He shall not immediately cease to pray. Rather his first prayer should be that he may regain his faith. His loss of faith, incurred perhaps by immersion in objections to theism or by a crisis in his life, may prove to be of short duration. However, all prayers to a hypothetical God have their limits beyond which they seem artificial or even hypocritical. All are mere shadows of true, full, and Christian prayer that presupposes both belief in God and (to anticipate the next section) an experience of him.

My next topic, then, is the relation between prayer and our experience of God. Before I discuss this I must state briefly a fundamental principle of religious epistemology that I have defended at length elsewhere.[5] We cannot base belief in God solely on reason or authority. So far as reason goes, the repeated criticisms of the theistic arguments have shown that they do not prove God's existence with rational certainty. Also we cannot base faith solely on authority. If the authority is a merely human one we can always query it and ask how we know that its testimony is true. If the authority is God or his word we can ask how we know that God exists or that he is speaking to us. Both reason and authority have their parts to play in the life of faith, but they cannot constitute faith's sole grounds. This is not only an epistemological necessity. It is also a religious one. As the Bible makes abundantly plain, God's purpose for us is not merely that we should know about him indirectly, by reason or authority, but that we should know him directly by experience, as a child knows her father or one friend knows another.

Yet although our experience of God is direct (as every experience must be) it is also mediated. Almost anything can mediate this experience. Within Judaeo-Christian theism the chief media are nature, the moral law, the history of Israel, the Liturgy, the lives of the saints, and (above all) the biblical testimony to Christ. We are not obliged to use the word 'experience'. We can speak instead of apprehending God, being conscious or aware of him, or simply knowing him (where we mean a knowledge of him 'by acquaintance', not merely 'by description'). However, 'experience' has these advantages. It includes everything that is signified by the other words; it invites comparison with non-religious forms of experience; and it is used in both religious and secular contexts to indicate a distinctive mode of cognition.

The relation between experience and prayer is a close one. Although the experience of God occurs in various ways through the media I have mentioned, it is unlikely to be sustained, or at any rate deepened, apart from prayer. In prayer we address God directly. We adore him for what he is, we thank him for his gifts, we confess our sins to him, and we ask him for his grace. In all these acts we approach God as a personal being who confronts us and with whom we commune. This is so for innumerable Christians who, although they may not reflect on the matter (as I am now doing), nevertheless find in prayer an unequalled way of making contact with God and opening their minds to him. These points here need noting.

(a) We must not isolate the experience of God we obtain through prayer from the experience we obtain of him by other means. The media of experience I stated can become occasions of prayer. The experience of God in nature leads to the praise of him as the creator. The experience of him through the moral law, by inducing a sense of guilt, leads to confession and a plea for his forgiveness. Chiefly, the experience of God in Christ leads to the adoration of the Trinity whom Christ reveals, to thanksgiving for the redemption that Christ brought, to confession of our sins in the light of Christ's obedience, and to supplication for the gifts that Christ bestows.

(b) Prayer yields an experience both of God's transcendence (his otherness) and of his immanence (his closeness). The coincidence of transcendence and immanence is one of the main elements in the theistic view of God. It can be experienced in many ways, but it is especially apt to be experienced in prayer. In prayer we are aware simultaneously both of God's transcendent majesty

114

that elicits our adoration and of his nearness to us through the Holy Spirit who inspires our prayers and conveys the life of Christ to us in response to our petitions.

(c) As I have just implied in my reference to the Holy Spirit, the experience of God in prayer reflects the trinitarian pattern that characterises prayer *per se.* In prayer we can experience each of the divine persons when we name them separately. But just as the dominant form of trinitarian prayer is addressed to the Father in the Son and through the Holy Spirit, so the correlatively dominant form of experience has this threefold character. The experience of God as Father can occur whenever we recite the opening words of the Lord's Prayer.

I shall return to the topic of experience later in this chapter. I shall next examine the language of prayer.

The language of prayer is of various kinds. It includes expressing, confessing, asking and asserting. We express our praise of and thanks to God; we confess our sins to him; we ask him for his gifts; and in all these forms of prayer we make assertions about him (mainly by ascribing properties to him). It is the assertive form that concerns me now.

In religious discourse as a whole the assertive use of language has two characteristics. First, in speaking to God in prayer, just as in speaking about him in other contexts, we apply to him both positive terms and negative ones. We apply positive terms when we address him as 'Thou' and endow him with a mind and will. This is further specified by the personal images we apply to him (as when we call him father, lord, and king). But in order to affirm his transcendent majesty we also apply negative terms to him (as when we call him infinite and immortal).

Secondly, in speaking to God in prayer, just as in speaking about him in other contexts, we use symbols both directly as analogies and indirectly as metaphors. The difference between the two types of symbolism is well illustrated by the beginning of the Lord's Prayer in its Matthean, commonly recited, version: 'Our Father who art in heaven'. 'Father' functions directly as an analogy. There are essential points of correspondence between human fathers and the divine Father. God exhibits infinitely characteristics that human fathers exhibit finitely. But 'heaven' is only a metaphor (albeit an appropriate one) for indicating God's transcendence. God does not inhabit a 'super' heaven beyond the sky we can observe; being pure spirit he is non-spatial.

These are genuine observations that affect all our speech about God. As such they would require expansion if this were a book on religious language. I shall deal next with two limited questions that concern the language of prayer and that have often been raised in recent decades.

Although the first question affects religious language as a whole, it has an especially acute bearing on prayer. It would scarcely have arisen forty or fifty years ago; but it has often been raised recently in the context of 'feminism' and 'feminist' theology. It arises from the so-called 'sexist' bias towards 'masculinity' inherent in traditional descriptions of God and particularly in the invocation of him as 'Father' in prayer. God is depicted as male rather than female; and this is held to express a male exclusion of (or even domination of) the female. In order to see this objection in perspective it is necessary to realise that it applies to all male descriptions of God, including such basic terms of reference as 'he' and 'him'. I maintain that a consideration of the following factors is sufficient for rebutting this objection.

(i) Although God himself, being infinite and incorporeal, transcends sexual differentiation, we are bound to call God either 'he' or 'she' when we speak of his (or her) personal character by analogy with our own human form of personality. If we speak of God solely as 'she' we replace a male preference by a female one. In order to avoid this we should need to speak simultaneously of both 'he' and 'she'. We should also need to combine male and female images on all occasions. However, to adopt such usages would be intolerably artificial, cumbersome, and often incongruous. (ii) Male descriptions of God are so deeply embedded in the language of the Bible and, as a consequence, tradition that to replace them by, or even combine them with, female equivalents would involve an unacceptable programme of linguistic revision. In particular we should be committed to altering the language that Jesus used both in his own prayers and in the prayer he gave to his disciples. (iii) The qualities of tenderness and care that are often held to be distinctively feminine ones are associated with God's fatherhood both in the Bible and in the Church's worship. (iv) Christians know God in Christ and they pray to God in the name of Christ. Now, Christ was a man, not a woman. Therefore male images (principally the image of Son) are inevitable in descriptions of Christ and of his relationship to God. (v) Within the order of redemption the distinctively feminine role is assigned to Mary who is superior to all human creatures (male as well as female) in being the 'God-bearer' (*Theotokos*).

The second question concerns the choice between the traditional 'Thou' and the modern 'You' as modes of addressing God in prayer. Reasons can be given both for and against both pronouns. In favour of 'Thou' there is its place in translations of the Bible (including the RSV and the NEB) and in the liturgy of the Church. Against it some would claim that, being an archaism, it stands in danger of suggesting, first, a dead rather than a living tradition and, secondly, a God who is remote from us and our concerns. In favour of 'You' it can be urged that, because it is currently used in secular speech, it is more effective than 'Thou' in bringing religious language alive and suggesting God's presence with us as our loving father. Against 'You' some have held that it is less effective than 'Thou' in eliciting reverence and awe. Doubtless these (and other) reasons for and against 'Thou' and 'You' will be variously assessed, so that different people will come to different conclusions. Since this is so, and since this is a minor matter, I suggest that in public worship both modes of address are permissible, and that in private prayer each person should adopt the mode that comes naturally to him or her.

Finally, we must not so far concentrate on language that we overlook the non-linguistic elements in prayer. I have already referred to these in dealing with the distinction between vocal and mental prayer. Even vocal prayer has mental aspects; and the final stage of mental prayer to which the mystics testify is wholly wordless. I shall now consider a further, particular, way in which prayer exceeds language. It occurs when, although we strive to pray, we cannot formulate our prayers or at least cannot do so adequately. Paul expresses it as follows with reference to the work of the Holy Spirit. 'In the same way the Spirit comes to the aid of our weakness. We do not even know how we ought to pray, but through our inarticulate groans the Spirit himself is pleading for us, and God who searches our inmost being knows what the Spirit means, because he pleads for God's own people in God's own way' (Romans 8:26–27, NEB). The NEB rightly notes that the words it renders 'how we ought to pray' can also be rendered 'what it is right to pray for'. The first rendering could be taken to mean that we cannot find the right words to express our prayers. The second rendering is more radical. In this case we do not know what is the right object or content of our prayers (particularly, it may be reasonably assumed, our petitions or intercessions). Then, although we are reduced to 'inarticulate groans', the Spirit pleads (or intercedes) for us through them.

Paul does not explain the nature of the Spirit's intercession. Also, there is no parallel elsewhere to these verses in his Epistles. In order to understand them we must remember that the Holy Spirit is always active in our prayers. He both initiates our prayers and, the more we submit to his influence, purifies them. This is part of his wider role as the one who presents us in the Son to the Father. When we are unable to formulate our prayers, the Spirit formulates them for us according to the mind of Christ; and as such they are accepted by the Father.

This can sometimes be a matter of experience. Christians sometimes obtain the experience of being (as it has been put) 'prayed through'. They are aware that it is not merely they who pray, but that it is also the Holy Spirit who prays through them. This experience can occur in two opposite ways. It can occur when we find ourselves inspired beyond our natural powers and when we feel that the right words are 'given' to us. It can also occur when we are unable to find the right words or when we are unsure what we ought to ask God for (or whether a request we have in mind is appropriate). It is the second way that Paul indicates here. And so I come back to the theme of experience on which I shall comment further in the following two sections.

My next topic is the role of feelings in prayer. This calls for distinctions between various senses that 'feeling' can bear. First, there is the question whether we need pray only when we 'feel like' it. The answer to this obviously is that we are obliged to pray, as we are obliged to worship, even if we do not feel like doing so. There are bound to be many occasions when we must overcome our lethargy or preoccupation with worldly things in order to spend time in prayer.

Secondly, there is the question whether prayer, once we engage in it, need be accompanied by specifically religious feelings. This question is connected with the first in so far as if we do not feel like praying we are unlikely to have religious feelings when we pray or at least when we begin to do so. Nevertheless, the second question requires treatment in its own right. Here it is necessary to comment further on religious experience as a whole. Our experience of God is often accompanied by such feelings as those of awe, contrition, joy, and being warmed or consoled by God's presence. It would be highly unusual for a Christian to lack these feelings entirely. Yet she need not always have them. It is possible to have a sense of God's reality without accompanying feelings or emotions. All this is no less applicable to the experience of God we obtain through prayer than it is to experiences of him that we obtain through other means.

The third sense of 'feeling' is one I have anticipated under the second sense, but it too deserves to be considered separately. I have given as one of the feelings accompanying the experience of God the feeling of being warmed or consoled by his presence. This feeling can accompany prayer, but it need not do so; and in the lives of devout Christians it often does not do so. Richard Harries states the truth thus:

> We should not try to force ourselves to feel one thing rather than another; in particular we should not try to induce the feeling that God is close to us. All that is necessary to begin a period of prayer is a pause, a moment of silence, a mental reminder that God is present as the unimaginable reality in whom

we live and move and have our being. If this mental act brings a feeling in its wake, well and good. If it doesn't, it doesn't matter in the slightest.[6]

Spiritual and mystical writers constantly tell us four things. First, we must not force ourselves to have religious feelings. Secondly, we must persevere in prayer even if we do not have them. Julian of Norwich summed it up thus in her fourteenth revelation: 'Pray wholeheartedly though you may feel nothing'.[7] Thirdly, we must expect periods of aridity in prayer, and indeed in our religious lives as a whole. Fourthly, in prayer we should seek not spiritual consolation for itself, but union with the will of God.

I pass now to a topic with which most writers on prayer feel obliged to deal. This consists in difficulties in, or obstacles to, prayer. These are many, but I shall discuss only the three main ones.

I have stated the first difficulty in the preceding section. We may find it hard to persevere in prayer because we lack religious feelings and, in particular, the feeling of God's nearness. It is on the latter feeling that I shall now comment. Sometimes God seems to be unreal, not in the sense that we have ceased to believe in his objective reality or even to apprehend it, but in the sense that we do not experience it as a presence irradiating and consoling us. It is as if God has withdrawn his light and warmth. We know him under a cloud that we are unable to dispel. This state is especially hard to endure when we contrast it with other periods in our lives when we have felt God's nearness to us.

When we find ourselves in this state we must recollect that mystics have undergone it to an intense degree. At the end even Christ underwent it, to judge from his cry of dereliction on the cross. If we undergo it in lesser forms and degrees we must continue to pray in remembrance of the times when God seemed near to us, in the hope that such times will return, and in the knowledge that God is in fact present with us even when we do not feel his presence. Furthermore, we can make our spiritual state into an occasion for prayer. Here is an example:

> O my God, thou art very near, in my heart and about my way; yet often thou dost seem very far off and my soul fainteth for looking after thee: thou dost lead me through dark places and withdrawest thyself from me. In the desolate time, when I feel perplexed and forsaken, I would think upon the cross of my Saviour and his dreadful cry, that my faith may hold fast in his faith and that despair may not seize me. Help me to remember the days of vision and sure confidence, guide me to stay my soul in the revelations of thyself which thou hast given me in time past through all thy prophets and servants, and bring me out of the valley of the dark shade once more into the light of thy presence, through Jesus Christ our Lord.[8]

The second difficulty in prayer is one that is often stated. This is an inability to concentrate. It can have many causes. It may be caused by tiredness, sickness or depression. In such cases a person will probably find it difficult to concentrate on anything. However, the cause that is most often discussed is mental distraction. A person finds his prayers interrupted by worldly thoughts; he cannot keep his mind fixed on God. Two initial things must be said to put this in perspective. First, even if we are in a physically fit state, and even if we are not worried or depressed, we often find it hard to concentrate on the task in hand. Secondly, distraction in prayer is experienced even by those who have progressed far in the spiritual life. Beyond these reflections we must take note of the following factors.

(i) Spiritual directors tell us it is unwise to fight distracting thoughts and try to expel them from our minds. If we do so they ate likely to persist or even increase. It is better to ignore them. They may then decrease or even disappear. (ii) If the distractions persist they can often be made into occasions for prayer. If we are distracted by a sinful thought or impulse we can make it a cause for confession and a cry for forgiveness. If we are distracted by a personal problem we can bring it to God and ask for his guidance. If we are distracted by thinking of other people we can intercede for them. (iii) Despite distractions our prayers are still acceptable to God if they are sincerely offered. (iv) If we find that distractions permit only a brief prayer God will accept the prayer if its motive and intention are pleasing to him.

Lastly, some people find it hard to pray or have even ceased praying because their prayers have been unanswered. Here I must refer back to my remarks on the so-called problem of unanswered prayer. There are many reasons why God does not always answer prayer. It is likely that some people see a problem here because they assume that the aim of prayer is to obtain from God what we want whereas its true aim is to conform our wills to his will. Again, they may have given priority to prayers for outward occurrences or material things rather than to prayers for the spiritual gifts that God is always ready to confer. These errors may also be accompanied by the false assumption that the power of prayer consists in and is verified by the extent to which our petitions and intercessions cause effects in the external world.

I shall deal finally with a group of questions that bear on the practice of private prayer. The questions refer to (a) the times, (b) the length, (c) the forms, and (d) the places of prayer.

There has been, rightly, a reluctance on the part of spiritual writers in recent years to give rigid and universally applicable answers to these questions. Conversely there has been a growing tendency to say that we must form our own style of prayer and be prepared to modify it if modification is required. At the same time there is widespread agreement that it is desirable for the Christians to adopt some rules of prayer to which they adhere as far as possible. Without this kind of self-discipline and perseverance it is easy for prayer to become infrequent and perhaps even to cease.

On the basis of these principles I suggest that the substance of the matter on each of these four questions is as follows:

(a) On the times of prayer it is self-evident that every time of the day or night can become an occasion for prayer. Nevertheless, there is a long tradition (in which many of us were instructed in our childhood) commending prayer especially in the morning soon after we awake and in the evening when we prepare ourselves for sleep. The tradition is a sound one. It is manifestly appropriate for Christians to commit themselves to God at the beginning and at the end of the day, to ask for God's guidance and strength for the coming day and to ask his forgiveness for sins committed in the day that is past. Apart from this tradition it is for each Christian to pray at those times that suit his or her circumstances and needs. I shall recur to the question of prayer's times when I bring this chapter to a close.

(b) The question of prayer's length is a complex one. Prayer may be preceded by or interwoven with meditation (which I shall discuss in the next chapter); and vocal prayer can pass into mental prayer. Therefore, the length of time we spend in prayer must not be limited to the time we spend in vocal prayer. There is no rule for the length of time we spend in prayer. A short time of undivided attention is better than a long time marred by distractions or spent as a discharge of irksome routine. In particular brief vocal prayers uttered with attention are better than longer ones that produce the defects I have just mentioned. The Lord's Prayer is a brief one, in accordance with Christ's injunction to avoid wordiness in prayer. Again, there is the short 'Jesus Prayer' that, though it has its origins in Orthodoxy, has been adopted by Christians of other communions. Obviously, the longer we are spontaneously drawn to spend in prayer the better. Yet frustration and disillusionment are bound to occur if we force ourselves to lengthen our prayers in the mistaken belief that the longer we pray the more spiritual we become and, thereby, the more pleasing we are to God.

(c) The question of prayer's forms can have one of two references. It may refer to the various forms of vocal prayer I examined in chapters 2 and 3: adoration, thanksgiving, confession, petition and intercession. Not all these forms need occur whenever we pray. Yet all should occur regularly. I have already said that petition is appropriate to the beginning of the day and confession to its end. In thanksgiving we must thank God for all his gifts. For this purpose the Anglican General Thanksgiving provides an incomparable summary. Furthermore, there are always particular things in our daily lives for which we owe thanks to God. In intercession, although we must remember the needs of the whole world, we have a special duty to pray for those whom we know in various contexts and relationships.

'Forms' may also refer to the distinction between prayers written by others and extempore prayers (by which I mean prayers that we ourselves formulate on the spur of the moment). Each form has a place in private prayer. On the one hand, every Christian can benefit from using prayers contained in the Church's Liturgy and in the many collections of private prayers written by individuals (such as, to take two outstanding twentieth-century examples, John Baillie's *A Diary of Private Prayer* and Michel Quoist's *Prayers of Life*). On the other hand extempore words are necessary for adding spontaneity to our prayers, for relating our prayers to our own circumstances, and (above all) for expressing the cries of the heart that are wrenched from us in moments of desperation.

(d) The question of the 'places' where private prayer is offered is also not amenable to any inflexible rule. The nature of the case, reinforced by the teaching and example of Jesus, requires us if possible to be alone (in a room of our home, in a church, in the open air and so on). Yet it can be hard, perhaps impossible, for a person to find solitude. He or she must then learn to pray silently in the company of other people. This brings me to a final observation that is, I hold, of major importance and that is relevant, not only to the places of prayer, but also to its times. Although Christians must reserve times and (so far as this is possible) places for prayer, they must also learn to offer brief prayers in the midst of life. The content of our prayers will depend both on our inner state and on our outward circumstances. It may be a prayer for patience if we know that we are about to meet an irritating person. It may be a prayer for chastity when we encounter an incitement to lust. It may be a prayer that we may speak the right words (as when we are about to visit a friend in hospital). These are all examples of petitionary prayer. Prayers of thanksgiving too must be offered in this way (for example, when we receive good news instead of the bad news we had feared).

Anthony Bloom gives the following example of a prayer for guidance in a particular situation.

> We may sometimes find ourselves in a group of people arguing hotly with no hope of solution. We cannot leave without causing further disorder, but what we can do is mentally to withdraw, turn to Christ and say, 'I know that you are here, help'! And just be with Christ. If it did not sound so absurd one would say, 'Make Christ present in the situation'. Objectively he is always present, but there is some difference between being there objectively and being introduced by an act of faith into a given situation. One can do nothing but sit back and just remain with Christ and let others talk. His presence will do more than anything one could say. And from time to time, in an unexpected way, if one keeps quiet and silent together with Christ, one will discover that one can say something quite sensible that would have been impossible in the heat of the argument.[9]

This passage shows two further things. A brief prayer uttered in the midst of life can pass into mental prayer consisting simply in the recognition of Christ's presence. Also the result of such a prayer is often silence on our part until we are moved to say something helpful that, without the prayer and the silence, we could not have said. Our words then are due to the Holy Spirit who proceeds from Christ and testifies to him.

CHAPTER SIX

FURTHER QUESTIONS (II)

In this chapter I shall deal with three topics: the ideas of meditation and contemplation, mystical prayer, and prayers to and for the dead. The first and second topics are related in so far as contemplation is often associated with prayer in its mystical forms. I have left the third topic until the end of the book for reasons I shall give immediately before I begin my discussion of it.

Prayer has constantly been related to, and sometimes even identified with, meditation and contemplation. Therefore, an independent examination of these two concepts is required. I shall base my remarks on the definitions of them given in the *Oxford Dictionary of the Christian Church*. I shall begin with meditation which the dictionary defines thus: 'As the term is used by exponents of Christian spirituality, mental prayer in its discursive form. It is the type of mental prayer appropriate to beginners and as such is accounted its lowest stage; and it is commonly contrasted with contemplation. Its method is the devout reflection on a chosen (often Biblical) theme, with a view to deepening spiritual insight and stimulating the will and affections'. The writer then refers to Ignatius

Loyola's *Spiritual Exercises* as a widely used method of meditation.

This definition identifies meditation with mental prayer. Although the identification occurs elsewhere, I shall later challenge it. Otherwise the definition is, I hold, acceptable. It follows traditional usage in maintaining that meditation is a lower stage of spirituality than contemplation. Meditation can be practised by ordinary Christians, whereas contemplation, at least in its more advanced forms, can be practised only by mystics. The definition is also correct in noting that meditation is 'discursive', and that it consists in 'devout' reflection. It is discursive because in it our minds move from one point to another in thinking about a topic or text and its meaning for us. It is devout because, being aimed at discovering the religious meaning of a text or topic for us and for our spiritual progress, it differs from the intellectual approach adopted by a scholar or historian. This fact is brought out by the statement that meditation aims at 'deepening spiritual insight and stimulating the will and affections'. There is, however, one element in meditation, as traditionally understood, that the definition does not mention. This is 'imagination'. Spiritual writers often advise us, when we meditate on the Gospels, to imagine ourselves present at the occurrences (especially the occasions when Jesus said or did this or that) that the Evangelists describe.

Various methods of meditation have been proposed. The method stated by Francis de Sales in his *Introduction to the Devout Life* is a good example. This work was meant for laity living in the world and pursuing secular occupations. In part one de Sales offers ten meditations on various themes. The first (on 'our creation') well exemplifies the pattern he advocates. We are to begin by placing ourselves in the presence of God. We recollect that God is present everywhere, but especially in the depths of our souls. There then follow 'considerations' (for example that God has raised us from nothing). Next there are 'spiritual acts and resolutions'. With reference to belief in God as our creator these include humbling ourselves before him and resolving no longer to exalt ourselves but to bear humiliations. We pass then to thanksgiving, dedication, and petition. We thank God for creating us *ex nihilo*, we dedicate ourselves as his creatures to him, and we pray for strength to fulfil the resolutions we have made. We end with the 'Our Father' and 'Hail Mary'. This method of meditation is a clear-cut one that is applicable to any biblical or doctrinal theme we may choose.[1]

I shall now examine two questions. First, is it to be expected that all Christians will practise meditation? Secondly, is meditation a form of prayer?

An answer often given during the twentieth century to the first question—an answer I endorse—is that formal methods of meditation of the kind commended by de Sales are not helpful to everyone, especially if the meditation is a prolonged one (and de Sales commended meditation for an hour a day). Some people may find such methods congenial, if not exactly as they stand, at any rate with adaptations to suit their needs. Others will find all methods constricting and arid. If, by a deliberate act of self-discipline, they embark on one, they may find that their minds wander, perhaps far more than they are prone to do in the normal course of vocal prayer. It is here worth noting that formal meditation has never been a part of Orthodox spirituality.

However, it lies within the scope of most Christians to meditate non-formally on religious matters. There is no need to adopt a formal method in order to practise meditation as the *Oxford Dictionary of the Christian Church* defines it (namely, 'devout reflection on a chosen theme, with a view to deepening spiritual insight and stimulating the will and the affections'). Non-formal, like formal, meditation can have many objects such as a divine attribute, God's acts in creating and redeeming us, a saying of Jesus or an incident in his life, his death and resurrection, the lives of the saints. The fundamental requirement is that we should cultivate a meditative attitude or outlook so that we find it more and more natural to dwell on thoughts of God, Christ, and their significance for us. In fact, all Christians whose faith is not of a superficial or merely passive kind practise non-formal mediation to some degree even if they do not call it meditation and even if they are unfamiliar with meditation of a formal type.

My second question, and the one that is more important for my present purpose, is whether meditation is a form of prayer. Meditation and prayer have often been identified. I maintain that the identification is invalid for reasons that apply to both vocal and mental prayer. First, there is the fact that meditation can occur in non-theistic contexts. Thus it is practised by Buddhists who do not hold the belief, essential to Judaeo-Christian prayer, in a personal God who is the creator of the universe. Again, even Jews and Christians can meditate on a passage of scripture or on a religious truth without engaging in prayer. Thus there is a distinction between the Psalmist meditating on the law and praying to God as the author of the law. This distinction exhibits the following difference between meditation and prayer. In meditation we 'think about' words referring to God, whereas in prayer we commune with God himself either by addressing him (in vocal prayer) or by wordlessly adoring him (in mental prayer).

Certainly there is a close connection between meditation and prayer. Meditation is akin to prayer in

CHAPTER SIX: FURTHER QUESTIONS (II)

so far as it is permeated by an elevation of the mind to
God, a desire for knowledge of him, and a readiness to
hear his word. Also, meditation can be combined with
prayer. This combination may be of a formal kind (as
in the method prescribed by de Sales). It can also be
informal. This happens when meditation leads to prayer
by a spontaneous movement of the soul. It happens too
when we pray meditatively (that is, by thinking about the
words we utter). This method of prayer, whereby we linger
over the words we say slowly, is commended by spiritual
writers for use by Christians who find formal methods of
meditation uncongenial. Meditation and prayer can be so
closely interwoven that it is hard to distinguish between
them.

Nevertheless, meditation and prayer are not identical
for the reasons I have given. On this again it is appropriate
to quote Anthony Bloom.

> Meditation and prayer are often confused, but there
> is no danger in this confusion if meditation develops
> into prayer; only when prayer degenerates into
> meditation. Meditation primarily means thinking,
> even when God is the object of our thoughts. If as a
> result we gradually go deeper into a sense of worship
> and adoration, if the presence of God grows so
> powerful that we become aware of being with God,
> and if gradually out of meditation we move into
> prayer, it is right; but the contrary should never be
> allowed, and in this respect there is a sharp difference
> between meditation and prayer.[2]

I pass now to the idea of contemplation that the *Oxford
Dictionary of the Christian Church* defines thus: 'As used by
modern religious writers, non-discursive mental prayer,
as distinguished from meditation. In so far as this stage of
prayer is held to be reached by the normal development of

the natural faculties, it is termed "acquired contemplation" (also "the prayer of simplicity"); but when considered as the fruit of supernatural grace, directly acting on the soul, it is known as "infused" contemplation'.

'Contemplation' is elsewhere used in the ways stated in this definition. But it is also used in either a narrower or a wider way. It is sometimes used more narrowly to signify only the second form of it stated in this definition (that is, 'infused contemplation' of a distinctively mystical kind). The mystics tell us that once they reach this stage they are no longer able to practise meditation. 'Contemplation' has also been given a wider sense in which it embraces the spiritual life as a whole, so that it includes acts of meditation. Thus of the three degrees of contemplation listed by Walter Hilton the first and second include meditation and other forms of discursive thought. Only in the third degree do Christians reach a wholly non-discursive mode of knowledge that Hilton describes in terms of a spiritual marriage between the soul and God. In the twentieth century Von Balthasar has maintained that all Christian prayer is rooted in the contemplation of the scriptural testimony to God.[3]

There are these points in favour of using 'contemplation' in the wider sense in which it includes 'meditation'. (i) In ordinary speech we use meditation and contemplation interchangeably. Thus we speak of someone as having either a 'meditative' or a 'contemplative' disposition. (ii) Meditation is not wholly discursive. It includes a non-discursive 'pondering on' its subject matter. (iii) Contemplation is more effective than meditation in indicating the objective reality of God. Meditation can suggest mere reflection on concepts and images. Yet the ultimate aim of meditation is to have a deeper knowledge of God himself. (iv) Contemplation suggests 'seeing'. And 'seeing' God in and through the media of his self-revelation is one way of describing the religious experience on which, for all Christians, faith is based.

Yet there are these points in favour of restricting contemplation to 'infused' contemplation of the kind that only mystics enjoy. (i) The word is thus restricted both by some mystics (such as the two Carmelites to whom I shall refer) and by some writers on mysticism (such as David Knowles). (ii) Mystical contemplation stands in contrast with meditation and is thus contrasted by the mystics themselves. (iii) The restriction of contemplation to its mystical form helps to underline the distinctiveness of mystical experience. Whether mystical contemplation can be validly regarded as a form of prayer is a question I shall discuss later. At any rate it is closer than meditation is to prayer in so far as it is a non-discursive awareness of God and of his presence in the soul. Mysticism will be my next topic.

My aim in this section is to examine mystical forms of prayer and to relate them to those forms that I have already examined and that all Christians can practise. But I must first comment on mysticism as a whole.

Mysticism is a complex topic for many reasons of which the chief ones are these. First, there is the question of what we mean by 'mysticism'. This term (like 'religion' in which it is an element) has been defined in a bewildering variety of ways. At one end of the scale mysticism has been defined so broadly that it includes almost any experience, or sense, of the divine. At the other end it has been so narrowly defined that it signifies only an advanced type of experience that has been obtained by only a few people. Secondly, there is the question whether, if we take a narrower rather than a wider definition of mysticism, we can detect various types of it. The third question, which is closely related to the second, concerns the similarities and differences between Christian and non-Christian forms of mysticism. It is only after we have answered these questions that we can properly answer the fourth question which is the one that bears directly on the theme of this book. This question is whether mystical experience can be included within the category of prayer.

For my present purpose I am compelled to answer the first, second, and third questions briefly although a much longer treatment is required by the questions *per se*. However, my answers accord with a large body of religious interpretation and linguistic usage. I shall take 'mysticism' in a narrower rather than a wider sense both because it is commonly thus taken by Christian theologians and because unless it were so taken there would be little or no difference between mystical and non-mystical Christians and so between mystical and non-mystical forms of prayer. Specifically, I shall take Christian mysticism to signify the various forms of experience that accompany the 'infused' mode of contemplation and that I shall later describe in detail. Yet I shall also urge that within Christianity there is likeness as well as unlikeness, continuity as well as discontinuity, between mystical and non-mystical types of experience and prayer.

With regard to the second question there are clearly various types of mysticism. These have been authoritatively examined by R. C. Zaehner in his *Mysticism Sacred and Profane*. Within the sacred, or religious, forms of mysticism the main types are the theistic and monistic (or pantheistic) ones. According to the theistic type the mystic claims to experience only a union of love with the transcendent creator from whom he remains ontologically distinct. According to the monistic type the mystic claims to experience actual identity with God or the Absolute. Next there is the distinction between the form of theistic mysticism found among non-Christians as well as

Christians and the distinctively Christian form based on God's revelation of himself in Christ. This leads inevitably to the question of the similarities and differences between Christian and non-Christian forms of mysticism.[4]

Many similarities can be discovered between these forms. The similarities consist partly in those mental states (such as heightened awareness, ecstasy, and bliss) that a variety of mystics claim to have enjoyed, and that are open to psychological description. Yet the main points of both similarity and difference between Christian and non-Christian forms of mysticism are of the metaphysical kind I have stated. The chief similarity is between the Christian form of theistic mysticism and non-Christian forms of it. The chief difference is between the theistic form of mysticism and all pantheistic or monistic forms of it. This is well brought out as follows by E. G. Parrinder in his *Mysticism and the World's Religions*.

> Here is the true distinction, between communion and union on the one hand, and identity on the other. Identification with God in the sense of 'Thou art that', or 'I am God', is rejected not only by Jewish mystics but by nearly all Christian mystics, by orthodox Sufis, and by monotheistic Hindus going back to Ramanuja and the *Bhagavad Gita*. This is the watershed in mysticism, not between prophecy and wisdom, or Semitic and Indian, but between theism and monism, between communion and identity.[5]

It has sometimes been maintained that all mystical experiences are identical and that mystics differ only in their later descriptions, or interpretations, of their experiences. This view has been widely criticised in recent decades.[6] It rests on an untenable separation of experience from belief. The experience itself differs according to the beliefs with which it is associated. A theist obtains one kind of experience that is shaped by theism whereas a monist obtains another kind of experience that is shaped by monism. A Christian mystic obtains further modes of experience that are shaped by the belief that in Christ the second person of the Trinity became man for our salvation. Only a theistic form of mystical experience can give scope for prayer that presupposes belief in a personal and transcendent creator whom we can address as Father, of whom we can make requests, and with whom we can enjoy a union of mutual love.

I come now to my fourth and last question which is whether mystical experience is a form of prayer. From now on I shall be dealing solely with the Christian form of mysticism. Christian mysticism can be and often is discussed without any reference to prayer. It is not uncommon to find writers describing the whole spiritual progress of the mystic through purgation and illumination to union without any (or with very little) reference to prayer. Yet according to the testimony of the mystics themselves the whole mystical way is a way of prayer subject to these qualifications. Mystical prayer is of a purely mental, non-verbal, and so non-vocal kind. It therefore lacks the element of petition. E. Allison Peers has expressed the coincidence of mysticism with prayer as follows with reference to the two Carmelites John of the Cross and Teresa of Avila.

> Prayer, for St. John of the Cross as for St. Teresa, is no mere exercise made up of petition and meditation, but a complete spiritual life which brings in its train all the virtues, increases all the soul's potentialities and may ultimately lead to 'deification' or transformation in God through love. It may be said that the exposition of the life of prayer, from its lowest stages to its highest, is the common aim of these two saints, which

each pursues and accomplishes in a peculiarly individual manner.[7]

If we ask what are the distinguishing characteristics of mystical experience and so of mystical prayer we shall not find clear-cut answers given by all mystics. Also, even when they do provide answers they do not always use the same language or draw the same distinctions. There are sometimes differences within the writings of the same mystic. Nevertheless, we find a fairly consistent answer given by the two great Carmelites I have mentioned. Mystical prayer, they affirm or imply, is supernatural; it is passive; it is infused; and it is a state of contemplation going beyond meditation. All these characteristics are brought together by John of the Cross in a brief passage contained in his *Ascent of Mount Carmel.* There he says that the mystic obtains 'a supernatural knowledge of contemplation'; that the soul reaches a state where 'God communicates himself to it passively'; and that 'this reception of light which is infused supernaturally is passive understanding'.[8]

Each of the preceding terms requires comment. All Christian experience is supernatural in the sense that it exceeds any knowledge of God that is obtainable through our natural, created, powers; it occurs through the action of the Holy Spirit who proceeds from the incarnate Son and testifies to him. Yet mystics claim to experience God in a mode that is supernatural in a further, special, sense. This mode is elucidated by the words 'passive' and 'infused'. 'Passive' signifies that mystical prayer is due, not at all to human effort, but solely to God's action in the soul; it is entirely infused as a crowning gift of grace. Finally, it is a state of contemplation in which the soul relinquishes discursive thought in general and meditation in particular.

Although Teresa does not use the precise, scholastic, terminology used by John of the Cross, she says more about prayer as such and, especially, about the stages of mystical prayer. She offers the following account of these stages in her *The Interior Castle*. First, there is the prayer of recollection, then the prayer of quiet, then the prayer of union, then the spiritual betrothal between the soul and God and finally spiritual marriage. Teresa illustrates the difference between non-mystical prayer (which is 'acquired' by human effort) and mystical prayer (which is 'infused' by divine grace) through the analogy of the different ways in which two water troughs are filled. One trough is filled through aqueducts by means of human skill and effort, while the other is filled spontaneously by an underlying spring. Teresa's stages of mystical prayer must not be rigidly separated from each other. One stage passes almost imperceptibly into, and is perfected by, the next stage. Thus the prayer of quiet is a more intense form of the prayer of recollection; and the state of spiritual marriage fulfils all preceding forms of union.

Nevertheless, it may be asked whether, despite the claims made both by the mystics themselves and by writers on mysticism, mystical experience (and so mystical contemplation) can be validly regarded as a form of prayer.

In view of, first, the place that vocal prayer occupies in Christian tradition, and, secondly, the universally strong association of prayer with speaking to God (and especially offering petitions to him), it may well seem surprising to include within prayer a wholly non-verbal, purely mental, state of contemplation. Yet the inclusion becomes intelligible and justified when we take account of these facts to which I earlier drew attention. All vocal prayer has mental aspects; the prayers of ordinary, wholly non-mystical, Christians can take purely mental forms;

all true prayer goes beyond words in being a contact with God; and the ultimate aim of petition is conformity to and union with the will of God through sanctifying grace. In her *Life* Teresa defines mental prayer as 'an intimate sharing between friends'. In the light of this definition and the preceding facts I stated we can see how mental, and specifically mystical, prayer is a deepening of the personal relationship with God that belongs to the essence of all Christian prayer. We must also note again that however far Christians progress in the mystical way their modes of prayer are accompanied by the vocal and petitionary prayers of the Church's Liturgy and supremely by the prayer that Christ himself gave to his disciples.

In assessing mystical prayer (and so, if we are going to use these terms, mystical experience and contemplation) we must attempt to strike a balance in the following respects. On the one hand, mystics experience forms of mental prayer that are not experienced by non-mystical believers and that deserve to be called, in a special sense, supernatural. On the other hand, mystical experience fulfils the experiences obtained by ordinary believers. When the latter pray they too can experience a communion with God that adumbrates the *unio mystica*. All Christians too can echo, even if in much lesser degrees, what the mystics signify by 'passivity' and 'infusion'. In prayer they can experience a new strength and a new illumination that are given to them by the Holy Spirit and that vastly exceed anything produced by antecedent efforts of their own.

The same complementary facts emerge from a consideration of the ways in which mystics and non-mystics experience God's transcendence and immanence. Christian mystics are acutely aware of God both as one who transcends them in his infinite majesty and as one who is present with them in the depths of their being. By his transcendence God surpasses their comprehension so that they can speak of him in terms of darkness as well as light; but because he is immanent in them he enables them to achieve the forms of union with him that are signified by the metaphors of betrothal and marriage. Although the mass of Christians cannot experience the mystical mode of this twofold experience, they can obtain a foretaste of it. They too, when they pray to God, can be aware of him both as one who utterly transcends them in his great glory and as one who is incomparably close to them as their father and friend.

Yet these judgements are all relative ones. However close we come to God in prayer (or in any other way) all our knowledge of God now (even the knowledge conferred by mystical contemplation) is immensely less than the knowledge we shall obtain hereafter. There is no exception to Paul's rule that 'now we see in a mirror dimly, but then face to face'.[9] Our last request to God, both for ourselves and for others, should be that at the last we, being perfectly united with him and with each other in his triune life of love, may enjoy the vision of him eternally.

The concept of eternity forms a bridge to my last topic: prayers for and to the dead. I have left this until the end for these reasons. First, whatever views we take of it we are bound to admit that prayer is primarily addressed to God or to Christ as his incarnation. Also our intercessions are primarily for the living and their present needs. Although our prayers must constantly be directed to the life to come, we pray primarily that we and others may so live now that we may be worthy of eternal life hereafter. Secondly, there is no explicit evidence for either prayers for or prayers to the dead in the New Testament. Thirdly, such prayers are largely absent from the Reformed stream of the Western Church. Nevertheless, their prevalence in the pre-Reformation Western Church, the post-Reformation Roman Catholic Church, and the Orthodox Church make a consideration of them inevitable.

On prayers 'for' the dead it is necessary to distinguish between prayers at a funeral when we pray for the deceased person and prayers for the dead as a whole. It is natural (I should say necessary) that prior to burial or cremation we should commend the departed to the mercy of God and pray that, his or her sins in this life being forgiven, he or she may find rest and peace. Such prayers occur in Reformed liturgies. The scope of our prayers here is limited to a once-for-all transition from this life to the next. Moreover, such prayers can be of a general kind; they need not specify the nature of the life to come. It is another question whether we can rightly offer further prayers for souls within their post-mortem existence. Here we must make further distinctions. I take it for granted that we cannot appropriately pray for souls in heaven or hell; for the final state of such souls has been irrevocably reached. This leaves us with purgatory.

Belief in purgatory was taken for granted in the Middle Ages; but it was rejected by the Reformers. However, although since the Reformation the belief has been a characteristically Roman Catholic one, some Protestants have treated it sympathetically and even held it in some form. Is it, then, appropriate to pray for souls in purgatory? Surely it is so. If we pray for those on earth who are on their way to heaven we can reasonably pray for those who are continuing the journey beyond death. Yet there is a difference between the two cases. We can validly pray for souls in purgatory that they may endure in hope the pains that their state entails. But we cannot validly pray (as we pray for souls on earth) that their pains may have a happy outcome; for this (their entrance into heaven) is assured. It is not necessary for us to make our payers for them precise. If (as I have maintained) a general form of words is sufficient in our intercessions for persons on earth, *a fortiori* it is so in our intercessions for souls undergoing a purgatorial process of which we now know nothing. It is enough for us to remember such souls before God and identify ourselves with his saving will for them.

In fact some prayers found in non-Roman sources imply some kind of intermediate state in which departed Christians are purified for entrance to heaven. Here is a prayer found in the B.B.C'.s service book *New Every Morning.*[10] The same prayer is also found, with only slight differences of wording, in the Anglican anthology entitled *Parish Prayers.*[11] 'O almighty God, the God of the spirits of all flesh, multiply, we beseech thee, to those who rest in Christ, the manifold blessings of thy love, that the good work which thou didst begin in them may be perfected unto the day of Jesus Christ'. The prayer then continues by linking the destiny of departed souls with the destiny of those who still live on earth. 'And of thy mercy, O heavenly Father, grant that we who now serve thee here on earth, may at the last, together with them, be found worthy to be partakers of the inheritance of the saints in light'.

Next there are prayers 'to' the dead. These were never meant to be substitutes for or equivalents to prayers to God. Rather they are requests to the dead to pray to God on our behalf. Traditionally prayers have been addressed to Mary, martyrs and saints. The best known prayer to Mary is the one beginning *Ave Maria* and containing the words, 'Holy Mary, Mother of God, pray for us sinners now and in the hour of our death'. The main grounds on which prayers to the dead have been justified are these. If we ask Christians on earth to pray for us (or for other people, as a minister may ask his congregation to pray for its sick members), *a fortiori* we can ask it of souls who are so much closer to God and who are perfected in charity. Indeed, if souls in heaven are aware of us they surely already pray for us, and especially for those whom they once knew on earth. If, too, the thought that those on earth intercede for us brings us comfort and strengthens our sense of belonging to the Church as the Body of Christ, *a fortiori* such effects can be produced in us by the thought that intercessions are offered for us by those in heaven. Nevertheless, even if prayers to the dead are (as I believe they are) justifiable on these grounds they are valid only if they fulfil the following conditions:

(i) We cannot validly ask the departed to pray on our behalf for material things or for one rather than another state of temporal affairs. We can validly ask them to pray only for our spiritual good, so that we, persevering to the end in their footsteps may at the last join their company.

(ii) We must be careful to avoid the error of supposing that the saints, because they are so close to God, can persuade him to show a concern for, or a clemency towards, us that he would not otherwise show. Especially in praying to Mary we must not think that she represents mercy, that Christ represents justice, and that in answer to our prayers she prevails upon her son to be merciful to us. On the contrary all Christian intercession is grounded in the love (and so the mercy) of Christ.

(iii) However close to God departed souls may be, they remain creatures who cannot confer the divine gifts for which we ask their prayers. Above all they cannot confer the divine salvation that Christ offers us through the Holy Spirit.

(iv) It follows that we must not allow our prayers to Mary and the saints to encroach on or diminish Christ's office as mediator. His mediatorial office is threefold. First, as one who was both human and divine, he mediated between God and man in his own person. Secondly, in his humanity he mediates divine salvation to us. Thirdly, through him we have access to the Father. In these ways his status as mediator is unique and all sufficient. It is unique: as the incarnate Son he mediates God to us as no-one else can do. It is all-sufficient: in him we have all we need for our salvation; and in him we have full access to the Father.

(v) Our whole attitude to Mary and the saints must be governed by the contrast between the 'veneration' due to them and the 'adoration' due to God alone.

In fairness to those who are in favour of praying to the departed it must be said that they often state these qualifications. Thus Roman Catholic theologians often deplore any opposition to the mercy of Mary to the justice of Christ. Such opposition is not found (to take a classical example) in Anselm's prayers and meditations. Moreover, his prayers make it plain that he assigns a place to Mary in the scheme of salvation only because she is the mother of Christ. His whole theory of the Atonement rests on the conviction that only Christ, as the God-Man, could do what was required for the reconciliation of sinners to God. With regard to the concept of mediation it is enough to quote the Second Vatican Council's statement, in its decree on the Church (*Lumen Gentium*), that the invocation of Mary as Advocate, Helper, Benefactress, and Mediatrix must be 'so understood that it neither takes away anything from nor adds anything to the dignity and efficacy of Christ the one Mediator'.[12] This should be taken together with the decree's earlier comment on Mary's 'influence on men'. 'It flows forth from the superabundance of the merits of Christ, rests on his mediation, depends entirely on it and draws all its power from it. It does not hinder in any way the immediate union of the faithful with Christ but on the contrary fosters it'.[13]

Prayers to the dead have often been regarded with suspicion and occasionally with abhorrence by Protestants. This has sometimes been due to ignorance of the ways in which these prayers have been qualified by Catholic theologians. This ignorance too has sometimes been accompanied by a failure to perceive, or at any rate to feel, the unity of the Church militant below with the Church triumphant above, although the unity is expressed in the New Testament (especially in Hebrews 11–12), in the Apostles' Creed's reference to 'the communion of saints', and in hymns that Protestants sing. Nevertheless, Catholics ought to take note of Protestant objections to prayers to the dead; for however adequately the objections may be answered in theory by the qualifications I have stated, the qualifications can easily be, and clearly have been, ignored in practice.

It is likely that Christians will continue to differ in their views on prayers for and to the departed. In order to see these differences in proportion we must take note of the following facts. First, the differences need not be absolute. Thus it is possible to approve of prayers for, but not of prayers to, the dead. In fact many within the Reformed tradition find it natural to pray (as their forms of liturgy often require) for the recently departed. The only question then is whether we extend our prayers beyond this to imply some kind of purgatorial state between death and the final bliss of heaven. Again, it is possible to offer simple prayers to Mary (such as the *Ave Maria*) without adopting further descriptions of her (such as the titles mentioned in the Second Vatican Council's decree). It may well be thought wise to avoid the latter lest they blur the uniqueness of Christ and the all-sufficiency of his saving work. Secondly, prayers to God and Christ are primary. The invocation of the departed (even of Mary) is of a secondary, derivative, kind in so far as their

147

prayers depend wholly for their meaning and validity on the salvation won for us by Christ as the incarnate Son of God. Therefore only prayers to God and Christ belong to the basis of Christian prayer. Thirdly, all Christians are united in giving thanks to God for the blessed departed and in asking him for grace to follow them as they followed Christ.

It is fitting that I should bring this book to a close with a summary of the relation between prayer and the hope of the life to come. This hope affects prayer in all its forms. It affects adoration in so far as the praise of God offered by the Church militant here below is a foretaste of, and is moreover invisibly united to, the praise offered by the Church triumphant above. It affects thanksgiving in so far as we thank God, first, for the immortality conferred on us by the risen Christ, and, secondly, for the inspiration afforded to us by the blessed departed. It affects confession in so far as we are obliged to confess that we have often sought our final good in this world instead of in the world to come. It affects petition and intercession (quite apart from prayers for and to the dead) in so far as we pray that we and others may see our lives in the light of eternity, endure our earthly trials in faith, and, by the sanctifying operation of the Holy Spirit, be made fit for the beatific vision.

I shall therefore conclude with the following two prayers. The first of them was written by Augustine.

> Blessed are all thy saints, O God and King, who have travelled over the tempestuous sea of this mortal life, and have made the harbour of peace and felicity. Watch over us who are still in our dangerous voyage; and remember such as lie exposed to the rough storms of troubles and temptations. Frail is our vessel, and the ocean is wide;

but as in thy mercy thou hast set our course, so steer the vessel of our life to the everlasting shore of peace, and bring us at length to the quiet haven of our heart's desire, where thou, O our God, art blessed and livest and reignest for ever and ever.[14]

The second prayer was written by the English poet John Donne.

Bring us, O Lord God, at our last awakening, into the house and gate of heaven, to enter into that gate and dwell in that house, where there shall be no darkness nor dazzling, but one equal light; no noise nor silence but one equal music; no fears nor hopes but one equal possession; no ends nor beginnings but one equal eternity; in the habitations of thy glory and dominion world with end.[15]

To the one eternal God, Father, Son, and Holy Spirit be ascribed all honour, glory, praise, and thanksgiving now and forever. Amen.

NOTES

FOREWORD

1. *Christian Theism: A Study in its Basic Principles* (Edinburgh: T&T Clark, 1984).

2. I can not help recalling what Borges said: '...The man who truly desires the disappearance of his books does not assign this task to others', 'Franz Kafka, *The Vulture*' in J. L. Borges, *The Total Library: Non-Fiction 1922–1986* (London: Penguin, 2001), 501. I mention these works in the hope that some reader of this volume who was a friend of Huw actually possesses a copy of one of these works and might be persuaded to bring it to light.

3. Although readers will probably find it most natural if I refer to 'Huw Owen' and he himself could make professional use of those words, I occasionally refer to 'Huw Parri Owen' because his middle name was always used when people referred to him in his native land of Wales. Because this sounds so cumbersome to the unfamiliar ear and 'Huw Owen' sounds so abnormal to the familiar Celtic ear, I occasionally refer to him by first name only.

4. I shall abbreviate titles from now on. Publication details are *RE* (Cardiff: University of Wales Press, 1957); *MA* (London: Allen & Unwin, 1965); *CD* (London: Macmillan, 1971) and *CKG* (London: Athlone, 1969).

5. *Sigmund Freud: Life and Work*, 2 vols. (London: Hogarth, 1955/6). Huw's self-confessed obsession with psychology during his later years at school probably owes a lot to this family connection.

6. London: Athlone, 1976. This, *Chistian Theism* and the four volumes in n.3 above are the six books produced during their author's lifetime. He also published several essays and articles pertinent to the theme of this present volume. 'The Sinlessness of Jesus' in S. R. Sutherland and T. A. Roberts, *Religion, Reason and the Self: Essays in Honour of H. D. Lewis* (Cardiff: University of Wales, 1989), for example, is not only valuable in its own right, but is also profitably read alongside the treatment of temptation in chapter 4.

7. *CKG* 251.

8. *CT* 111. He refers to von Hugel in this connection in *CKG*, loc. cit. My impression is that he was increasingly persuaded of von Hugel's position after the publication of *CT*. The reader is well advised to follow up the actual essay in von Hugel's volume, to which Huw Parri Owen makes reference in *CKG*.

9. *The Personal God: Is the Classical Understanding of God Tenable?* (Carlisle: Paternoster, 1998), 6. At least, he holds that this is the case as far as the volume written by Clark Pinnock and others goes: *The Openness of God: A Biblical Challenge to the Traditional Understanding of God* (Downers Grove, IL: InterVarsity Press, 1994).

10. Discussion of prayer is integrated into the author's wider theology in *CT*, chapter 4.

11. He died, we recall, almost a decade ago. It is true that, even in his own day, Huw Parri Owen engaged less with contemporary theologians and trends than did many of his peers. Some of the thinkers to whom he refers in this present volume have, by now, largely dropped out of sight, for example, his former colleague in King's, H. D.

Lewis, whom he mentions alongside Keith Ward and Richard Swinburne in chapter 1, n.7. Lewis refers to three of the works in question in the preface to a fourth volume, *The Elusive Self* (Basingstoke: Macmillan, 1982). When, at the beginning of his volume, Huw makes reference to most Christians being familiar since infancy with the Lord's Prayer, he rather evokes a world that has, to some degree, passed away.

12. *CT*, chapter 7.

13. I confess that I have been intrigued by this, but never drew him out very far on this judgment. Possibly he took for granted that right-thinking people would simply ignore what Calvin said, for example, about the Roman Catholic Church. It is worth adding that he was also, I think, more impressed by Barth than his writings suggest; I say this not because of a judgment about the theological proximity of Calvin and Barth but to indicate that Huw Owen's sympathies might occasionally be rather wider than his writings seem to indicate.

14. *CT* 119. My own description of libertarian freedom is less careful, but I cannot expand it here.

15. By 'rational', I do not mean just something to do with logical deductions. It comprises our supposed intuitive grip on the reality of human experience.

16. Reference to the 'Cartesian individual' is sometimes all too glibly made in these days, in a critical way. Nevertheless, I think that it is presently apt. Descartes (1596–1650) was a hugely significant figure in the development of Western thought and the adjective 'Cartesian' takes its name from him. It is his kind of rationalism and individualism that is in view here.

17. A very rare example where I have ventured to modify a point of substance occurs at the end of the second paragraph of chapter 2. Where the present reads that 'the Church has sometimes distinguished between

the adoration (*latreia*) due to God and the veneration (*douleia*) appropriate to the saints', the original text does not use the word 'sometimes'. I have made this correction because it looks as though Huw is saying that the whole Church standardly makes this distinction, as the next sentence suggests that we standardly venerate the saints. I have made it only because I believe that Huw would have been happy with this amendment. Strictly speaking, there is a more precise way of amending the wording, but it would take us too far from what the author himself wrote.

18. *Most Moved Mover: A Theology of God's Openness* (Carlisle: Paternoster, 2001), 95.

19. *CT* 137.

PREFACE

1. George Appleton, ed. *The Oxford Book of Prayer* (Oxford: Oxford University Press, 1985).

CHAPTER ONE: THE NATURE OF PRAYER

1. John of Damascus, *De Fide Orthodoxa* (3.24) in *A Select Library of Nicene and Post-Nicene Fathers, Vol. 9* (Oxford: Parker, 1899).

2. Karl Rahner, *Sacramentum Mundi: Concise Edition* (London: Crossroad Publishing Company, 1977), 1275.

3. Walter Hilton, *The Ladder of Perfection*, Leo Sherley-Price, trans. (London: Penguin, 1957), 30–35.

4. David Knowles, *What Is Mysticism?* (London: Sheed & Ward, 1967), 81.

5. Daniel Rees, ed. *Consider Your Call* (London: SPCK, 1978), 284.

6. Gordon S. Wakefield, ed. *A Dictionary of Christian*

Spirituality (London: SCM Press, 1988).

7. Although the soul's distinctness from the body has been challenged by various forms of materialism and behaviourism, it has been vigorously defended in recent decades by such Christian philosophers as H.D. Lewis, Keith Ward, and Richard Swinburne.

8. Michael Walker, *The God of our Journey* (London: Marshall Pickering, 1989), 26–27.

CHAPTER TWO: FORMS OF VOCAL PRAYER (I)

1. Richard Harries, *Turning to Prayer* (London: Continuum, 1978), 33.

2. John Macquarrie, *Twentieth-Century Religious Thought* (London: SCM Press, 1963), 215.

3. Revelation 5:12.

4. Quoted in Appleton, ed. *The Oxford Book of Prayer*, 3.

5. Psalm 100:4.

6. John 3:16.

7. Romans 8:28.

8. I John 1:8-9.

9. I Corinthians 13:3.

10. Psalm 51:4.

11. In F.L. Cross, ed. *The Oxford Dictionary of the Christian Church* (Oxford: Oxford University Press, 1963).

CHAPTER THREE: FORMS OF VOCAL PRAYER (II)

1. Thomas Aquinas, *Compendium Theologiae* (St. Louis: B. Herder, 1947), 248.

2. Matthew 7:7.

3. Matthew 21:22.

4. Matthew 7:11.

5. Mark 14:36.

6. John 15:7.

7. 1 John 3:22 and 5:14.

8. William Temple, *Readings in St. John's Gospel* (London: Macmillan, 1952), 302–306.

9. Thomas Aquinas, *Summa Theologiae, Vol. 39* (London: Blackfriars, 1963).

10. Mark 10:38–40.

11. D. Z. Phillips, *The Concept of Prayer* (London: Routledge & K. Paul, 1965), 125–126.

12. Thus Paul's intercessions for his churches are all prayers for spiritual blessings. See, as examples, I Thessalonians 5:23; 2 Corinthians 13:7; Philippians 1:9-11; Colossians 1:9ff.

13. Thus the N.T. records prayers for the sick (e.g. in Acts 28:8) or commends such prayers (as in James 5:14-15). Again Paul prays for a safe journey to Rome, and he asks the Romans to pray for his deliverance from the unbelievers in Judaea (Romans 1:10 and 15:30-31).

14. Thus in James 5 prayers for the sick are associated with the forgiveness of sins. Paul too prays, or asks prayers, for his safety solely in order that he may fulfil his apostolic mission. The only place where Paul is said to pray for a temporal blessing for himself is 2 Corinthians 12:8 according to which he asked the Lord for deliverance from his 'thorn in the flesh'; but the Lord answered 'My grace issufficient for you, for my power is made perfect in weakness'.

15. For example, I Kings 3:9-14 affirms that God was pleased with Solomon because he prayed for wisdom, not material things.

16. W. E. Pollard, *Chance and Providence* (New York: Scribner, 1958), 75.

17. H. H. Farmer, *The World and God: A Study of Prayer, Providence and Miracle in Christian Experience* (London:

Collins, 1935).

18. John Baillie, *The Sense of the Presence of God* (Oxford: Oxford University Press, 1962), 64–65.

19. George Appleton, *Prayer in a Troubled World* (London: Darton, Longman & Todd, Ltd., 1988).

20. Peter Baelz, *Prayer and Providence* (London: SCM Press, 1968), 115.

21. William Barclay, *Testament of Faith* (London: Continuum, 1975), 47–48.

22. Luke 23:46.

CHAPTER FOUR: THE LORD'S PRAYER

1. Thomas Aquinas, *Summa Theologiae, Vol. 39* (London: Blackfriars, 1963).

2. Joachim Jeremias, *The Prayers of Jesus* (London: SCM Press, 1967).

3. Galatians 4:6 and Romans 8:15–17.

4. John 1:12–13.

5. Ephesians 4:6.

6. Hebrews 12:9.

7. James 1:17.

8. I Corinthians 8:6.

9. Matthew 11:25.

10. A. M. Hunter, *Design For Life* (London: SCM Press, 1960), 68.

11. Ezekiel 36:23.

12. C. F. Evans, *The Lord's Prayer* (London: SPCK, 1963), 32–33.

13. Matthew 12:28.

14. T. W. Manson, *The Sayings of Jesus* (London: SCM Press, 1949), 169.

15. Quoted in Appleton, ed. *The Oxford Book of Prayer,* 96.

16. Mark 8:34.

17. Matthew 4:4.
18. John 6:27.
19. Matthew 6:31–33.
20. Matthew 6:15.
21. Luke 18:13.
22. James 1:13–14.
23. James 1:2–3.
24. Op. cit., 170.

CHAPTER FIVE: FURTHER QUESTIONS (I)

1. E. G. Jay, *Origen's Treatise on Prayer* (London: SPCK, 1954).

2. M. F. Wiles, *The Making of Christian Doctrine: A Study in the Principles of Early Doctrinal Development* (Cambridge: Cambridge University Press, 1967), 87.

3. St. Anselm of Canterbury, *Complete Treatises, Vol. I*, J. Hopkins & H. Richardson, eds. (London: Edwin Mellen Press, 1974).

4. For another statement of the view that it is reasonable for agnostics, but not for atheists, to pray see Brian Davies, *Thinking About God* (London: Geoffrey Chapman, 1985), 329–330.

5. H. P. Owen, *The Christian Knowledge of God* (London: Athlone, 1969).

6. Op. cit., 92–93.

7. Julian of Norwich, *Showings* (New York: Paulist Press, 1978), 249.

8. A prayer composed by W.R. Matthews and quoted in Appleton, ed., *The Oxford Book of Prayer*, 129.

9. Anthony Bloom, *Living Prayer* (London: Darton, Longman & Todd, Ltd., 1990), 56–57.

CHAPTER SIX: FURTHER QUESTIONS (II)

1. Francis de Sales, *Introduction to the Devout Life* (London: Hodder & Stoughton, 1988).

2. Op. cit., 51.

3. Hans Urs von Balthasar, *Prayer* (London: SPCK, 1973).

4. R.C. Zaehner, *Mysticism Sacred and Profane: An Inquiry Into Some Varieties of Praeternatural Experience* (Oxford: Oxford University Press, 1957).

5. E.G. Parrinder, *Mysticism in the World's Religions* (London: Sheldon Press, 1976), 119–120.

6. Notably in two volumes edited by Steven Katz: *Mysticism and Philosophical Analysis* (London: Sheldon Press, 1978) and *Mysticism and Religious Traditions* (Oxford: Oxford University Press, 1983).

7. E. Allison Peers, *The Complete Works of St. John of the Cross* (London: The Newman Press, 1964), 1.

8. Ibid., 120–121.

9. I Corinthians 13:12.

10. British Broadcasting Corporation, *New Every Morning: The Prayer Book of the Daily Broadcast Service* (London: British Broadcasting Corporation, 1948), 104.

11. Frank Colquhoun, ed., *Parish Prayers* (London: Hodder & Stoughton, 1988), 203.

12. W.M. Abbott, ed. *The Documents of Vatican II* (London: G. Chapman, 1966) 8.62.

13. Ibid., 8.60.

14. Appleton, ed. *The Oxford Book of Prayers*, no. 413.

15. Ibid., no. 547.

www.ingramcontent.com/pod-product-compliance
Lightning Source LLC
Chambersburg PA
CBHW032100080426
42733CB00006B/359